FROM HERE to HAVING IT ALL
in NETWORK MARKETING

Ken Dunn

ISBN: 978-1-934919-11-8

More Heart Than Talent Publishing, Inc.

6507 Pacific Ave #329
Stockton, CA 95207 USA
Toll Free: 800-208-2260 FAX: 209-467-3260
www.MoreHeartThanTalentPublishing.com

Cover art by FlowMotion Inc.

Printed in the United States of America

This book is dedicated to my father, Allen Dunn, who lost his life when he lost a battle with Lou Gehrig's disease at the age of fifty-four. My dad gave his entire adult life to the service of his country. He taught me every day about commitment and hard work. As I travel the world today, I carry his driver's license with me as a constant reminder that he is with me.

It is because of the lessons that I learned from my dad that my family enjoys the freedom we do today.

I am donating the proceeds from this book to the Canadian ALS Society in memory of my dad.

Acknowledgements

I would like to thank the many people through the years who periodically reached out to me and tried to help me to see that I needed to become a better person. Your efforts did not go in vain.

Most importantly, I want to thank my best friend, my partner and my love, Julie. Thank you so much for always encouraging me and for sticking with me and supporting me, even in the darkest hours. *Love, Laughter, and Friendship...*

To my beautiful kids, Matthew and Laura:
I love you both so much. You make me smile and laugh so much. Everything I do in my life is for you. My favorite thing in the world to do is to play with both of you.

Special thanks to Steve Scott, Fred Ninow, and Greg Fullerton:
Thank you so much for trusting me with your company and your family. You three men are a true inspiration to me. I'll never be able repay the trust and support that you have given to me.

Finally, to the few people that truly stuck with me over the past several years:

I am indebted to you for life. I will never forget your support and loyalty.

Table of Contents

Introduction   9

1. My Journey   15

2. How Being Introduced to Gandhi Changed My   39
    Life

3. Three Types of Leaders   57

4. Finding a Great Mentor   65

5. Prospecting: Your Core Task   79

6. Have a Why That Makes You Cry   115

7. Improve Your Communication   127

8. Build Confidence   137

9. Pay Attention to the Details   145

10. Create a Gravitational Pull   157

11. Serve Others   171

12. Live in the Now   179

13. Just Do It - A Call to Action   187

     Recommended Reading   197

Introduction

This book is not another personal development story published to help further a career. Nor was it written to inflate my ego or increase my reputation. I wrote *From Here to Having It All in Network Marketing* as a public accountability statement. During the past five years, I have had to completely redesign my personality. I have had to totally change who I am. I have decided to publish the story and the facts to set the record straight and to hold myself accountable as I continue on my journey.

Six years ago, I was one of the most detested people I knew. Through a series of events, I realized how terrible my outlook on life was, how flawed my personality was, and how terribly I treated other people. Once my flaws were thrown into the open, I set a course to completely revamp myself. My goal was to create wealth for my family, to create stronger friendships and relationships, and to become a better person.

In my book, you will learn how I personally received guidance and mentoring from some of the world's elite leaders: Bill Gates, Warren Buffett, Steve Jobs, Mahatma Gandhi, Mother Teresa, John F. Kennedy, and Pierre Trudeau. From their examples, I found the person that I wanted to be.

As I started to work on becoming a better person, my entire life became better, our family income increased, my circle of loyal friends increased, and my relationships became stronger.

The road to becoming a better person and ultimately becoming an inspirational leader has been a long and painful one, but at the same time it has been the most exhilarating journey of my life. I decided to write *From Here to Having It All in Network Marketing* to keep myself accountable. You see, I am not the inspiration to others that I hope to be... YET! One of the hardest things in the world to do is to change habits and personality traits. Publishing this book publicly holds me accountable and forces me to continue on the journey to becoming better.

There is another, deeper reason that I have decided to publish this book. Over the past five years, I have traveled all over the world and met thousands of people. In my journeys, I have met many people who had an incredible desire to create success, who desperately wanted to change their lives. When I got to know these people, I was able to easily identify personality traits that were holding them back from achieving that success.

Every one of us has personal habits and traits that don't serve us well. Whether it is constantly interrupting others, talking too much, rambling on, not truly caring about others, not telling the truth at all cost, etc., *From Here to Having It All in Network Marketing* will force you to take a closer look at your own life, determine what personal traits and habits you have that could be potentially holding you back, and learn how to fix them.

I am sure that some of you in reading this book and learning about all of the challenges that I have had with my personality will realize some of your own limitations. This book will show you how those little issues and subtle flaws could be the biggest reason for your lack of success to date.

Introduction

Finally, I know that as you read this book, you will think of someone that has the same challenges that I have gone through. It can be very difficult to point out areas where other people need to improve themselves. We are caring folks and don't want to offend others. We also have this "don't want to get involved in other people's stuff" mindset, so we would never point out where someone else might need to make improvements in their personality. So when you are reading the book, when my story makes you think of a friend who may have some of those same challenges in their personality, GIVE THEM THE BOOK!

Prior to starting my first network marketing business, I was a police detective investigating murders, and at the same time I was running my own mortgage company with nine full-time employees and hundreds of millions of dollars in revenue. I joined the network marketing industry in 2003 on the urging of a friend.

In my first year in the business, I earned over *eighty thousand dollars*. Now, you may think that in itself is a great success story, but there is a darker side to the story. In my first year, I built my business with a police detective's personality. I had been a cop my entire adult life, and I had developed a very dark, egotistical, self-centered, controlling personality. As you can imagine, I built my network marketing business with that same personality.

Fueled by a dictating, controlling, and self-centered first mentor in the business, I became one of the most hated leaders in my company. I built the business the way my mentor did, by using fear, retaliation, and control. At the end of my first year in the business, two of my key leaders quit. Now, when your two biggest leaders quit your business, so does 90 percent of your business, and that's what happened to me! The first couple of days after they quit were the most painful days of my life. I cried, withdrew into my own world, and felt very alone.

As I came out of the haze, I realized that I had to become a better person. I went back to these two leaders and three other people in my life and asked them to point out everything wrong in my personality. Wow, what a painful experience that was! They gave me a list of *forty* things I had to change. I didn't know anyone could have forty things wrong with them!

A short time later, through an innocent Easter gift from my wife Julie, I was dispatched into a study of seven of the world's most influential leaders. As I studied these seven inspirational leaders, I saw ten personal characteristics emerge that they all had in common. I realized that if I just focused on these ten characteristics in myself, my entire life would be transformed – and it has been!

As you read *From Here to Having It All in Network Marketing*, you will learn the *ten traits of inspirational leadership*. You will also learn how to apply these traits to your life and FINALLY achieve the success you are looking for.

As you read, you will see how each of these icons in our world identified the *core task* in their life and then focused all their energy on that *core task*. You will also learn in the chapters of this book that the *core task* in our industry is *prospecting*. You will finally know how to make prospecting automatic in order to achieve the lifestyle you're looking for.

One of the biggest things I've realized during my journey in network marketing is that there is too much emphasis on personal development too soon. Before you get sucked into the personal development abyss, you have to get good at prospecting. In this book, you will learn the secrets to second nature recruiting. You will see how I have created an endless list of leads, and you'll learn why follow up is truly NOT the most important thing.

Introduction

How would you like to have a list of ten traits to focus on for the rest of your life? If you focus on the ten traits of inspirational leaders, then you will finally achieve the success you're looking for. How do I know that? Because I did!

As you read through the chapters of this book, you will learn how to create your own *gravitational pull*. When you walk into a room, your presence will captivate everyone. You will finally understand why it is so important to create a more likeable personality and how to do it.

You will learn why *mentorship* is so important, and you'll learn how to pick the right mentor for you. As well, you will know what to watch for and how to stay away from the wrong mentors. Some mentors could ruin your life if you don't know what to watch for (just ask me – it happened to me).

As you read *From Here to Having It All in Network Marketing* and learn about everything that I have been through on my road to a seven-figure annual network marketing income, think about your own journey and apply these same ten traits to your life. You will finally understand why personal development is so important and how to develop yourself without defocusing on the core task. I am positive that if you apply the ten characteristics of inspirational leadership to your life, you will create the dream lifestyle that you are looking for.

1

My Journey

Like many others, my journey in entrepreneurship is a "rags to riches" story, beginning when I was a child in Halifax, Nova Scotia. From the time I was young, I've always been the ultimate dreamer, even being the oldest of three children growing up in a pretty poor environment with my younger brother and sister. Although he did the best he could, our dad worked for the Canadian navy his entire adult life, and working for the Canadian navy didn't pay him very well.

At a very early age, I knew exactly what it felt like to be broke. Because of this, I know what it feels like today for so many families who are stuck in that same place. I remember Christmases when my folks couldn't even afford to buy Christmas presents, and I remember sneaking downstairs at 2:00 a.m. to find my dad sitting in the living room crying because there were just two or three presents under the tree. So I guess you could say I came from fairly humble beginnings. I mean – a highlight for us was having fried baloney for dinner on Wednesday nights!

As a kid in grade school, there were opportunities to go on class field trips to some pretty cool places – Spain, for instance, and other trips overseas to Europe. My family could never afford to send me, so I never went on these trips. Instead of traveling with the students in my class, I'd be put into a lower grade for the week, where I'd be tormented, made fun of, and criticized by the other kids.

Our family was so poor that my folks couldn't afford to buy clothes for all of us, so we took advantage of the Salvation Army. I would wear sneakers until I had literally worn holes through the bottom of them. I was so embarrassed when the other kids ridiculed and made fun of me for wearing shabby hand-me-downs that by the time I was twelve I began stealing clothes. This was the year when all the kids were wearing Converse basketball shoes, those red-and-white high tops. This was back in the days of Doctor Jay, and everybody was wearing them, except me.

As a dreamer, I always looked for a way to change my present situation, and in this case, I created an "exchange program" where I would actually walk into the department store wearing my old sneakers, try on a new pair of sneakers, and then just walk right out again wearing the new shoes.

One day I walked into the department store, tried on a pair of new high tops, and then I walked out with them on, leaving my old shoes behind. As I was leaving, a guy came up and grabbed me by the arm, saying, "I'm with department store security. I need you to come with me." I saw my life flash before my eyes and knew that when my dad found out life as I knew it was going to be over. I was scared to death.

The security officer pulled me back into the office and sat me down. He started to interrogate me and said, "I know you stole those watches. What did you do with them?" He had no idea that I was wearing the department store's sneakers – instead, he thought I had stolen something else. I adamantly denied stealing the watches, sweating bullets the whole time. Then my dad, a very stern military man, showed up. The security officer began to tell him what had happened. Finally, my dad and I were free to go when they realized I had nothing to do with stealing the watches, and we walked away (I was still wearing the new shoes from my "exchange program").

That moment saved my life. For many children that get away with things like this at a young age, it's the beginning of a career in crime. I spent fifteen years in police work where I saw that for many kids minor theft was where it all started, and their careers in crime progressed from there. But I was different; that day I decided that I needed more, and that I was going do something to earn the things I wanted honestly. I knew I couldn't steal anymore.

I'm not proud of this part of my history, and the only reason I'm mentioning it is to give you an idea of the pain from my past that fuels my "why" and drives me in this industry today.

The Disease of Entrepreneurialism

When I was sixteen, I got a job working in a gas station, pumping gas. At seventeen, I overheard the owner of the gas station talking about needing to buy a tow truck and how he didn't want to go through the pain of managing it. I convinced him to let me buy the tow truck. He cosigned the loan for $100,000, and I began driving a tow truck every day to school. I used to skip classes to tow cars. I used to carry one of those big, old, clunky, black, size-of-a-BlackBerry pagers. Remember them? They used to go off with a loud *beep-beep-beep-beep-beep*. My pager would go off in the middle of physics class, and I'd get up and leave to tow a car.

The first year driving that tow truck around part-time, I earned more money than my dad did for our family. I was able to contribute a bit to the family lifestyle, and this is when the disease of entrepreneurialism first appeared in my life. I've been cursed with it since. I've always dreamed of a better life. This is my "why." In network marketing we are always told that we need to have a strong "why," and we're going to talk a lot about what drives people and the importance of having a strong reason for what drives you later on in this book. The thoughts that I've just described are the thoughts that drive me every day of my life; they are my "why." My desire is not to ever let any of my descendants go through the same experiences I did.

You know, there have been many books written and many studies done that suggest that, for the most part, generations of people are the same. I remember in law enforcement, you could go back ten generations of fathers and sons, and they were all cops. Or a son becomes a certified public accountant because that's what his dad is. Generations of women in the same family were nurses or doctors. Statistics show that more often than not, you will become what your father or mother is. In his book, *Becoming a Better You*, Joel Osteen had a big impact on me. He said that even though that's the way it is, people have the ability to break the cycle by deciding to take action to stop whatever the generational recurring pattern is.

In my family, the recurring pattern has been poverty. It wasn't just my dad. My grandfather was a plumber and battled with money his whole life. He and my dad had bad lines of credit and were in debt over their heads. Years before I read Osteen's book, I decided that I was going to break that cycle of poverty in my family, so I drove the tow truck through the rest of high school. Obviously, driving a tow truck every day during high school meant that I managed to miss most of my classes. I barely graduated from high school, and I really had no interest in pursuing further education. I wanted to make more money, but I didn't know what kind of job I could get to make the type of money I wanted to make. I didn't have a dollar sign attached to the amount – there was just no way that I wanted to live like I had when I was younger. I hated being ridiculed. It's been twenty-five years, and I still remember so clearly how I was made fun of by other people because of the clothes I wore when I was a child. It still plagues me that I could not go on those field trips, and I'm glad that it does. I hope I *never* lose those memories, because they humble me and remind me of why I must stay focused.

There are many heartfelt reasons for writing this book. One is to set the record straight – when it comes to success, I don't think age matters. In fact, I hate even telling people how old I am because there's always a stigma as soon as they realize my age. Many people have a hard time believing that somebody can really achieve multiple seven-figure income results before they are forty. I want this book to be the proof that I've been through as much, if not more, pain and suffering as anybody else. I just decided to expedite my exit from the pain and suffering, *and so can YOU!* Luckily, through this entire five-year process, I've made notes, I've had recollections, and I've been able to put it all into a process. I've identified a success track for people to truly become wealthy in network marketing, regardless of their backgrounds.

My Career in Law Enforcement

I knew I didn't want to drive a tow truck for the rest of my life. But I didn't have a clue about what I could do instead after high school. I certainly was not the most scholarly guy in high school. I was definitely never expected to be successful in life. I still have my high school yearbooks, and a couple of my buddies wrote in the back of one of my them, "Most likely to end up in jail." You never know where life is going to take you. Look back through your own high school days. Isn't it funny how the people we expected to be doctors and lawyers are blue-collar workers, and those we expected to fail are successful? Maybe desire truly can make dreams come true…

At the end of my senior year, the school held a career day, and we were all forced to attend. The Halifax police had a booth there; they were recruiting. I started asking them questions, and they said, "Well, you have to be twenty-one." They told me to check back in a couple of years. Right next to the Halifax police, there was a booth for the Canadian armed forces, and the recruiter overheard me talking to the Halifax police officer. The military recruiter said, "Well, would you think about the military police?" I had no idea what they were.

The long and short of it was that I ended up joining the Canadian military police when I was eighteen years old, and I became a police officer. Coming out of the training, I went right into investigative work. I spent my first couple of years in law enforcement investigating very significant drug trafficking. I did a lot of undercover work in my first two years. Industrial drug trafficking is not your typical idea of what you think military police would be involved in – you'd think it would be something to do with the war and military – but I had a really different experience. I did that for four-and-a-half years in total. From there, I moved to another city in Canada and spent the next three years working in a local police department with a SWAT team. I spent three years in tactical policing. We did all kinds of things like armed ship boarding, drug entry – really amazing things.

During this time I met my wife, Julie. She's my inspiration and my best friend. She's managed to put up with me, stick with me, and motivate me through these last five years. I met her at my cousin's wedding in Lindsay, Ontario. Julie was just finishing her nursing degree at Ottawa University in Ottawa, Canada, and we hit it off, fell in love, spent hours and hours talking on the phone in the beginning, and then she moved with me to Charlottetown, Prince Edward Island, where I was policing at the time. We stayed there together for a couple of years, and then I ended up moving to Ottawa, Canada, where I became a police officer with the Ottawa police service.

The funny thing was that during this whole time, I was still doing entrepreneurial things. This entrepreneurial fever just seems to boil through my blood. For fun, I used to write franchise proposals, businesses that I thought would do well. A few times, I actually wrote franchise proposals (unsolicited, of course), and sent them off to the franchises, and later, two of the businesses (which I discovered were privately owned companies, not franchises) ended up taking my advice and opening stores in the city that I had suggested. Of course, I never made a cent from it, but I've always had some really strong entrepreneurial blood in my body, although I didn't fully realize it at the time.

A Baby Changes Everything!

Things really changed for me when I turned thirty. My wife and I had a beautiful house on four acres in Ottawa, Canada. The house was worth $400,000. My son was born on July 15, 2001. Your life changes instantly the minute you see your first child. It is such an incredible, humbling experience. The first thing I thought as I stared at my newborn boy was, "You're going to have a better life than me. I am going to make that happen for you."

Prior to my son being born, I thought I was bulletproof. In my first ten years in law enforcement, I did a lot of undercover drug work. I was on a SWAT team; I saw many, many people die. During this time, nothing ever bothered me; I was never worried about my own safety. But the minute my son was born, I realized that I wasn't some superhuman being – I bled, and I could die. I ended up taking life a whole lot more seriously, literally overnight. At the time, I was investigating a murder, and I observed the devastation of that family's loss. I attended the funeral of the man who was murdered, and seeing his two-year-old son, I couldn't stop crying. It was amazing how my entire emotional state changed as a result of Matthew's birth. If you're a parent, you know what I mean. I began to realize that it was time for me to get out of police work. I was thirty years old, and I didn't want to do it anymore.

The other side of the story was that I had $100,000 saved up $100,000 in consumer debt, that is! I was living the Canadian/American dream. In Canada, cops are paid very well, especially detectives because they learn an amazing amount of overtime. I was making over $100,000 a year, but I was spending $120,000 a year. We had a $400,000 home with a $300,000 mortgage, two brand-new cars (both leased to the max), etc. I'd get paid on Friday, and by Tuesday I'd be broke again. I don't know how the heck it happened, but history was repeating itself; I was becoming my father's son. Does this sound familiar to you? It's incredible how many people in North America are living the same way.

I remember managing to pay two of the credit cards and the lines of credit, making the minimum payments on them, but then as soon as I got the minimum payment on one line of credit, I'd take it out again to pay the other credit card. Or I'd pay as much as I could and then go into an interview with the police credit union and get one of the lines of credit increased so I could make my car payments.

And then Christmas would come. I mean, how pathetic was Christmas for me? I know it is possible that some of you will stop reading the book when you read this sentence because you're living this right now. You know, you get through Christmas, and you've accumulated all that credit card debt. Everything you buy is on credit cards. Then you spend the next six months trying to pay them off. This was the life I was living. I realized when my son was born that I hated my job, and I wanted a change. I didn't *really* hate my job – I loved the work. I just wanted more. I was sick of the environment that I was in, and I was tired of making great money and being broke.

So I did what many typical Americans do when they realize they hate their job and want something more – I went out to look for *another* job. I didn't have any education outside of law enforcement, and $100,000 is a lot of money to replace. I guarantee that some of you will have a tear in your eye when you read this, because you're in that same boat right now. I've found out since then that this is the way most Canadians and Americans live every day. The best thing I could find was running security at a hospital for $40,000 a year. How could I ever make ends meet? During that period of time, one night I remember sitting on the corner of my bed. My wife was asleep. My little son, Matthew, was asleep. I sat on the corner of my bed and cried. I had no idea what I was going to do – absolutely none. I wanted so desperately to have a better life, to create a better life for my family, but I felt lost and alone.

New Opportunities

When I first moved to Ottawa, my wife and I lived in a condominium, and we paid condo fees. We had to pay $300 a month in our condo for our contribution to the grounds maintenance, etc., and it drove me crazy because there was very little actually being done. We were in a seventeen-unit building. I went to the condominium corporation and said, "Pay me the money, and I'll take care of all of the renovations, cut the grass, and everything." Then an idea popped into my head, "Well, what if I get a couple more of these condo buildings and start doing this for more people?" Luckily, in law enforcement I worked a schedule that consisted of four days on, four days off. This allowed me plenty of time to start a part-time business. I could manage that. I went out and pitched myself to a couple more condominium corporation boards and ended up having three different condominiums to take care of with almost eighty units. I was making about $15,000 a month in the beginning.

The Best Education Is Practical Experience

What started off as a great idea to create extra money on the side eventually became a nightmare for me, because I got so busy that I had to hire somebody else to do the snowplowing, hire somebody else to cut the grass, and hire a handyman to do the maintenance in the buildings while I was managing the entire operation. I was bringing in $15,000 a month in revenue, but by the time everybody else was paid, I made $500 a month, and I was working my tail off. My solution was to sell that business, and I made some really great money. This was an amazing learning experience in hiring other people to do the work and learning how to leverage my time and energy. I knew that it wasn't working properly, but it was a really valuable experience.

I was struggling along, and I started to open a few really neat businesses. I realized that if I was going to fix my problem with poverty, I had to open a business. I couldn't find a job that would pay me enough, so the answer had to be working for myself. Why would I want to spend all my time making someone else rich, anyway? I had no idea about what it was like to open a business. I had no idea about the owner being the last one to get paid and all that stuff. But I had it set in my mind that I'd have to open some type of business to make a fortune.

A couple of months later, a friend of mine came back from Mexico. While he was there, he found out how inexpensive sterling silver is if you buy it from the source. I went back to Mexico with him, and we visited a city call Taxco (sounds like "tasco"), the place where all the sterling silver jewelry is actually made. Big, bulky silver chains that sold for hundreds of dollars in the U.S. and Canada could be purchased from the manufacturer for five to ten dollars. We saw the business idea right away.

We came back to Canada, got an importer's license, and started importing and selling the jewelry. Within a year, we had imported over $2 million of sterling silver jewelry into Canada; we were making incredible money. I was making four times more money in this business than I had in law enforcement, and I was beginning to get some of my debt under control.

It was a great business, but again I was working like crazy. (I was still working full-time in law enforcement.) I was also a bit nervous because of potential issues with NAFTA (North American Free Trade Accord). I decided to sell my share of the business, which ended up being a profitable decision for me.

The Course Is Set...

A few months later, in 2002, right around Christmas, my personal banker paid me a visit at home in Ottawa. She saw how successful I was with my silver business and my property management venture, because she saw all the revenue we were bringing in with the silver business. Sabah had gotten into the mortgage industry and was a regional sales manager for a mortgage company in Canada called Home Loans Canada. She came over to my house during Christmastime because she was recruiting more mortgage brokers. We were good friends, but on this visit, she came over with a couple of beautiful pictures for our house, presents for the kids, and some really great cards for me, more than she'd ever done before. I knew she wanted something, but I wasn't sure what. She asked me what I thought about getting into the mortgage industry. I told her I couldn't leave my job, and she said, "No, I just want you to start part-time." We started joking around, and our joking got almost confrontational in a fun way. I was thirty-one years old, very cocky, and when she told me the types of incomes that the top guys in the company were making, I said, "If I do this, I'll be the top guy in this mortgage company in my first two years."

In 2002, the mortgage market was on fire. Real estate prices were very inexpensive. I had an unlimited database: there were 1,000 police officers in the police department who all trusted me. I've realized that one of the most important virtues in life is trust, and I had it exemplified there. I sent out an email to everybody through an interoffice email broadcast announcing that I was now able to arrange mortgages for them. In my first month in the mortgage industry, I earned about $18,000 – and this was doing it very part-time. By the end of the first year, I had to hire an assistant to process the mortgages; we actually funded over 25 million dollars in mortgages, and my family made just over $300,000 – again, this was part-time. It was unbelievable.

The business kept ramping up; I hired four full-time brokers to work for me in the second year, and my income doubled. In 2003, I became the top broker in Ontario in my province with Home Loans Canada. I funded around $40 million in mortgages. Things were going great.

My Introduction to Network Marketing

In September 2003, network marketing entered the picture. My wife and I had decided that at the end of 2003, if everything kept going the same way with my mortgage business, I would quit the police department and just walk away, because we didn't even need the money. All my debt had been paid off, and things were going well. A friend of mine got involved in a network marketing business, selling nutritional supplements, and he wanted me to get involved. I told him he was absolutely crazy. There was no way in the world that I was ever going to get involved in network marketing, direct sales, or whatever you wanted to call it.

Back in 1999, while I was a police officer, I worked in a fraud investigation where we investigated pyramid schemes. During the investigation, we had to study network marketing companies. We had to be able to differentiate in court between what was legal and what was illegal. I had the chance to attend some legitimate network marketing companies' meetings. We sat in the back of the room and listened to the speakers and watched what they were doing and how they were acting. I used to lean over to my partner all the time and laugh and say, "If I ever join one of these network marketing things, just shoot me." That summed up my attitude towards network marketing.

I was a really arrogant police officer. I was the typical cop. I thought all network marketers were loony. I thought it was all just absolutely silly. These people would stand up in front of a room and tell people, "If you follow your dreams and float on air, you can become rich." I thought they were loopy; I thought they were totally out to lunch. They were overly positive. They were trying to be these perfect people, caring more about others than themselves. I was the typical cop: arrogant, egotistical, and self-centered. (I want to make sure I qualify this by saying that I know all cops are not like that; I'm just generalizing.) I had a real strong personality. I just couldn't believe. I knew how hard I was working in conventional businesses, and I was there with a very skeptical mindset because I had to understand what it was all about so that I could say in court what was illegal and what was legal.

Once I was at a Mary Kay meeting, sitting in the back row, and I couldn't believe this woman up on stage. There was a Cadillac in the room, and she was a National Sales Director. There were about 200 people in the audience, and through the whole presentation, I felt like she was staring at me. We were just there to check the business model out and make a few notes, but I could feel her looking directly at me the entire time. I leaned over to my buddy and said, just joking around, "I think she's after me. She's going to make me join this thing."

The presentation ended, and I noticed that at some point my buddy had disappeared. Now, at these big presentations, what typically happens is that the speaker gets down off the stage, there's lots of handshaking, a few pictures, maybe an autograph or two. Well, in this case, the speaker made a beeline right to the back of the room, heading straight for me. She grabbed my hand and said, "I don't know who you are, but your being here is a testament to how badly you want to make changes in your life. I'd like to make you one of the first men to drive a pink Cadillac." I couldn't believe it! Needless to say, I had a really negative, uneducated opinion of network marketing. But I thought it was an educated opinion because I was there in the room.

When my friend John approached me about network marketing, I was totally focused on my mortgage business. John, who was in real estate, didn't think I would be interested in it, so he waited for several months before he invited me to take a look at it. What he did, though, was to refer all his clients to me. From his referrals, I was making over $20,000 a month – so you can bet that when John finally did ask me to take a look at his business, there was no way I could say no. John introduced me to his upline, Chris Gingras, who became one of my very best friends. He was the upline leader in that company. He was John's coach and had introduced John to the business. I came to a meeting were there were six guys, all of them with big checks showing all the money they had made, and Chris was the guy drawing the lines and circles. I had no interest in being there. It was just a big joke to me. While Chris is drawing out the circles and lines, I was answering phone calls, dialing numbers, and walking away during his presentation, but Chris stayed patient the entire time. I walked away from it – I didn't really have a clue what it was all about. Chris showed me the compensation plan, and two days later, John asked me to join and I agreed. Even though I had no real interest in it, I was intrigued, and I liked John.

I was busier than you could possibly imagine. I was investigating a murder at the time. On the side, I was running a mortgage company with nine full-time employees, doing hundreds of millions of dollars in sales. And then network marketing came along. This is a really important part of the story.

In network marketing we talk about systems and how to do the business. But I've always been an independent thinker. If I get a thought in my mind, I do it – and I do it my way. That has sometimes cost me a lot of money, but it's also made me some great money. I enjoy being an independent thinker.

When network marketing came along, I wasn't even sure if I was going to take it seriously. Since John really wanted me to get involved, I used to just call up my buddies and say, "Hey, I found a business opportunity. My buddy John got me involved in it. It's a network marketing company. I don't really care if you join or not, but I want you to sit down with John and hear about it so he'll leave me alone."

The guys that I talked to sat down and looked at the business; John explained it to them. Most of the time, I wasn't even there. Out of the eight guys I talked to in the first month, seven of them joined the business. I was blown away by this, but I had no idea what I was into. When I started to take it seriously was when I got a check for $2,800! I couldn't believe how little effort I put into making that type of money.

Now it all made sense. I had flashbacks to those seminars I sat through when I was a cop and what that Mary Kay lady said on stage. It all made sense now, and I started to study the model. In my fourth month in network marketing, my wife and I earned over $10,000, and I quit my job at the police department. My buddies at work all made fun of me, and some of them still do to this day.

Whenever I had an idea, I would always look for somebody who was ultimately successful in that field, whether it was the mortgage business, importing, or property management, and I'd get them to give me some advice on what they did to become successful – and then I'd just do what they said. I looked for someone like that in network marketing right away, too. I was very, very lucky, because my local upline happened to be a guy who was making $100,000 a month in network marketing.

Advice from the Top

We continued to build the business. After about five months, I had made $25,000. The guy who was making $100,000 a month in network marketing invited me to a generic training in Houston, Texas. At this event, I met leaders from all over the industry – people like Mark Yarnell, Tom "Big Al" Shreiter, Richard Brooks, Michael Clouse and Paula Pritchard – and I had the chance to spend some time with each of them. I told each of them the same thing: "I want to earn $100,000 a month. I want to become a millionaire in network marketing. What do I need to do?"

They gave me some really simple advice:

1. "Our business is about introducing new people. At all costs, never stop introducing new people."

2. "You must grow as a person. You must develop personally. This is a personal development business. Be somebody who's always learning. Read lots of books, and do everything you can to develop who you are personally."

3. "If you're in an international company, then build an international business."

I took this advice to heart, and by the end of my first year in network marketing, I had made just over $70,000.

40 Situations to Change

Everything was going great, or so I thought. One day, two of my top reps, who were also my friends, came over to my house to talk to me. They said, "We quit." I was shocked – I couldn't believe what I was hearing. These guys were making good money, too. And what was their reason for quitting? *They hated me.* I was absolutely beside myself. I had no idea.

They went on to say that the man who was mentoring me was a villain who was just in it for the money, and they felt that I was developing the same personality as him. They walked away, and about 90 percent of my downline quit because of this. I'll be really honest, I cried for a couple days. It was a very humbling experience to have somebody else lay it all out on the line and tell you what a terrible a person you are.

Those guys pointed out some really serious flaws; they told me that I was becoming a dictator, and I began to see that they were right. If you weren't with me, you were against me. I'd look people in the face and say, "The reason you're failing is because you're no good at this," and tell them to quit. I had fallen head over heels in love with network marketing, but I realized that if I were going to be successful, it would require change on my part. The only thing my friends didn't tell me was *how* to make those changes.

I have since learned a lot about what good mentoring is, which I'll cover in a separate chapter on this topic, but what I began to realize about this mentor was that my friends were correct. He *was* an absolute villain – in fact, he's known throughout the industry this way. He would belittle me on the phone. He would never allow me to be an independent thinker. And this is a volunteer army that we have here. He would call me up with one of his top guys on the phone because he didn't like the fact that I was going to go off and do something on my own, and he would criticize me to the point that I was in tears on the phone in my first year of network marketing. This was my first encounter with someone like this. And the worst part was that I *was* becoming more and more like him.

I've apologized to as many people as I can that were in my business in the first year because that's the way I became just following him. Throughout my whole life, I've always found somebody that has the success that I want and followed them. I've taken whatever they've done and tried to do it even better. But this was my first mentor in network marketing, and it was an unbelievable experience. The reality was that at the end of that first year, I was accused of becoming just like this person, and my accusers were right.

Because I recognized that I would have to change, I decided to talk to two men that had known me for more than five years, two people that had known me for less than five years, and I talked to my cousin. I said to them, "Hey, this is what's happened. I'm looking for some direction. I have no idea what to do. I want you to take the gloves off and tell me what requires improvement in my life, because I really require some assistance with this."

This is still difficult to talk about for me, many years later. These individuals each gave me several areas that required improvement, and I ended up with a list of *forty* things that were wrong with me. Talk about eating humble pie! I served myself up about six pies in one shot. It was mortifying. But at least now I knew the things that I had to change because I wanted to be better. However, I had no direction. I had nobody to work with, because I subsequently hammered that mentor; I confronted him and told him I literally wanted nothing ever to do with him again.

I believe that everything happens in life for a reason, and I believe that good things come to good people. There's a book that I read a while ago by Stephen Post and Jill Neimark called *Why Good Things Happen to Good People,* and I believe that's the case. I was trying to figure out how to do network marketing, I had this long list of things that I needed to improve on, and I realized that hammering people and beating them up all the time is not the way to do it. But what I learned about network marketing is that every single day is a new day. You have a chance to start again every day that you're in this business.

A List of Forty Things that Sucked about Me

As I mentioned, I asked several people to honestly share with me areas in me they felt required improvement.

I talked to two people that knew me for more than five years.

The first person:

- Arrogant
- Egotistical
- Self-centered
- Argumentative
- Controlling
- Ignorant
- Didn't care about other people

The second person:

- Self-serving
- Demanding
- Too aggressive with others
- Used foul language

- Abrasive
- Condescending

I talked to two people that knew me for less than five years:

The first person:

- Didn't care about others
- Money-focused
- Moody
- Belligerent
- Control freak
- Dictator
- Greedy
- Bad personality
- Self-serving
- Pushing too hard

The second person:

- Talks too much
- Puts others down
- Argues too much with others
- Always pointed out others' weaknesses
- Loses patience too fast
- Needs to be more relaxed
- Too uptight
- Too controlling

My cousin:

- Too tenacious
- Too aggressive
- Too hard on other people
- Arrogant
- Money-hungry
- Decisions are all about myself
- Greedy
- Self-centered
- Belligerent
- Pushes others too much
- Doesn't care about anyone else

Every Day Is a Fresh Start

Another rep of mine lived in Mexico. He asked me to do a three-way call with a man in Mexico named Juan Carlos Barrios. Juan Carlos had built a diamond distributorship in one of the biggest network marketing companies in the world in Mexico. He's an amazing leader, and in fact, he built his diamond distributorship during the very year that the Mexican currency was devalued. He created a massive residual income in spite of a very tough comp plan, making over $50,000 a month at the height of his career with this company. He was making millions of dollars in that business.

My rep in Mexico arranged for me to speak to Juan Carlos on the phone about expanding our business in Mexico. Because he and my rep were friends, Juan Carlos Barrios joined our business but never did anything. I flew down to Mexico City about a month later to meet with Juan Carlos Barrios and my friend. When I met Juan Carlos, I met a human being that was unlike anybody I've ever met in my life. He's one of the most pleasant, open, friendly people I've ever met, and we talked for hours and hours. We talked about where we came from, the similarities in our lives, etc. I forgot all about the business. During a four-hour conversation, I never told him about our business at all or the money I'd made.

We ended up building a really significant friendship in the coming months and years, and it all started from that one conversation. Juan Carlos, after that meeting, came back into the industry and went to work. Within six months, he had built the largest downline in Mexico in our company, and I was flying back and forth to Mexico every month to support him. This was the kind of mentor that I was looking for.

What you'll find is that mentors will come into your life at times and in ways that you wouldn't expect. I had realized that I didn't know how to love people. I never told Juan Carlos Barrios this, but he was all about love, and he built very strong allegiances in his groups. He taught me how to openly love and express yourself to others, how to show them that you really do care about them, and how to praise people and build the business through passion.

In my life, I had this devastating experience, I had these forty points to work on, and in a totally unconnected area, Juan Carlos Barrios comes along and begins teaching me about people and how to be a better person. Even though he was in my downline and I was his upline, he was always praising me and telling me what a great person I was. I observed how he interacted with people and how everybody loved him. He's just an amazing human being. He built a big business, we built an incredible friendship, and along the way, he taught me what love is all about.

Then on Easter in 2005, my wife (who I can never say enough about – and when she reads this, I want it to be another way for me to express to her how much I love her and owe her for sticking with me through all these experiences) knew that I was making changes because of all this stuff going on in my life, and she bought me a stencil, a little thing on a piece of plastic with a Popsicle-stick-like device to rub it onto the wall. The stencil, the saying, was from Gandhi. I'm looking at it right now as I write this. I still look at it ten times a day. Gandhi's quote is: "You must be the change you wish to see in the world." That one quote, that one small gift – maybe she gave it to me as a sign of appreciation, maybe she saw it and knew I was changing and saw how relevant it was – whatever the reason, the fact that she put that into my life has done amazing things, and this is where my journey intensifies.

2

How Being Introduced to Gandhi
Changed My Life

"You must be the change you wish to see in the world."
MAHATMA GANDHI

When my wife gave me that little Gandhi quote, it was just a tiny little gift, but it had a dramatic impact on my life. When I looked at it for the first time, it struck me deeply right away. It was the first time that I'd ever really understood anything about Gandhi. I knew he was a religious leader, and I knew he'd been through a lot of strife in his life. I knew he'd been persecuted throughout his life, but I never really understood his significance. That saying – that gift from my wife – was the absolute pivotal point in the complete shift to where I am today.

Before I got that little gift, I had started to see what my problems were. I had tremendous pain over the realization that I had a lot of changing to do if I was to become the person I so desperately desired to be. I had a mentor who gave me an idea of the bad side of the pendulum, and I'd begun to see the good side with heart-driven leaders like John F. Kennedy. I still didn't have any idea how to make the changes I wanted to make in my life, and then my wife gave me this stencil. I can't begin to express the emotional impact this saying had on me.

Even before I knew anything about Gandhi, that saying blew my mind. It really hit me considering what was going on in my life at the time. I'd lived through a really poor upbringing in my own life, and I was determined to do better for my kids. I knew that I had been a terrible person and I wanted to do better, and Gandhi summed it up in one quote.

I think Gandhi meant much more by these words, "You must be the change you wish to see in the world." My interpretation is that you have to be the catalyst for any change you want to see in your life, in your world. Everybody has issues. Everybody has trials that they go through all the time, but as many people that I've studied and learned have demonstrated, you *can* make those changes. You *can* break those trends in your family, in your generation. If there's something about you that you don't like and you want to make it different, you can change it. This quote has become synonymous with Gandhi and is known around the world, but I think it means that anything you wish for, you can have, as long as you're the catalyst to make it happen. That's the way I took it, and it became a real inspiration to me.

This one small gift from my wife led to a large desire within me to study as many incredible leaders as I could. Reading and rereading that quote gave me guidance and allowed me to put together a ten-point list of items that I began to focus on (and plan to focus on for the rest of my life).

Mahatma Gandhi

Because of this quote, I began to do some research about Gandhi. I wanted to find out everything I could about him. As I studied him, I was amazed at who Mahatma Gandhi was. Yes, he was a religious leader, but what stood out to me was his perseverance – his tenacity was incredible. He was persecuted by many, when all he was trying to do was praise and worship his God. Yet in spite of the persecution, millions of people followed him. He didn't own anything, but he was rich beyond his wildest imagination.

Mahatma Gandhi has become known as one of the most pivotal figures in Indian history in the twenty-first century. He encouraged Indians to boycott the sale of British goods. From the day he was born, he was always pushing for the things he absolutely believed in. He condemned corrupt governments. He condemned dictators. He stepped out on a limb for the people that he loved, and he was persecuted in the process. He was imprisoned. He was cast aside. Yet, in spite of everything, he never spoke ill of others. He stayed true to his beliefs – his beliefs in religion, his beliefs in independence, etc. Because he believed so strongly in his religion, he pushed for freedom in the practice of that religion. Gandhi was so instrumental in assisting India to become what it is today that it cost him his life. There was an initial assassination attempt on Gandhi's life on January 20, 1948, and then, just ten days later, he was assassinated by a fanatic. Fifty years after his death, he is still loved by millions of people, and his impact lives on.

He never spoke ill of others. He was imprisoned. He was cast aside. In spite of that, he stayed true to his beliefs – his beliefs in religion, his beliefs in independence. When I studied Gandhi, I found out that he attributed some of who he was to great guidance from his mentors. Gandhi served other people in an incredible way. He didn't care about wealth. He didn't care about riches. (He did care about prosperity, though, which is significant.) He cared deeply about other people. He had an unstoppable ability to get out there and create change. There was nobody else willing to do what he did, and he took action for no other reason than a strong inherent desire and belief.

Mother Teresa

My study of Gandhi led me to study Mother Teresa, and from there I studied other leaders in religion, politics, and business. That's how I developed a short list of ten things that I wanted to focus on for the rest of my life. (You'll find this list at the end of this chapter.) For me, this is where things really started to take off. Things began happening that were way beyond my own personal control.

I don't know how many of you have had a chance to really understand Mother Teresa, but what I learned about her was absolutely amazing to me. She won the Nobel Peace Prize in 1979. She won more awards than any religious leader, although she never asked for or sought any of them. She was persecuted her entire life, and although many people loved her to death, others absolutely didn't. I would argue that she might be one of the most influential business, political, or religious leaders of the world. She spent most of her life striving to assist the poor, and most people remember her for the amazing work she accomplished in Calcutta. Many world governments tried to persecute her for what she was doing, in spite of her completely unselfish service to others. Mother Teresa didn't have a cent to her name during her life, but she was definitely one of the richest leaders in the world.

Mother Teresa had a core task that she focused on every day of her life: worshipping her Lord and assisting the less fortunate. From the age of eleven or twelve, Mother Teresa felt a strong calling from God. She knew from a young age that her place in the world was being a missionary to make the love of Christ known around the world; this was her core task. At the age of eighteen, she left home and became a nun in an Irish community of nuns who did a lot of work in India. This was an amazing calling for her. And what were her reasons for what she did – what was her "why"? It would make even the darkest, most cynical person in the world cry. Her why was her love for God and her desire to assist the less fortunate, and for the rest of her life she never deviated from this. She just did it; she took action. Mother Teresa had an incredible gravitational pull: If she was ever seen in public anywhere, thousands of people came to her. It was amazing. How about communication? This simple, unassuming nun was incredibly articulate and enabled all kinds of people to understand her message. She built trust like nobody else. She always gave credit to God and to other human mentors that assisted her; she openly gave credit to others. Her whole life was dedicated to serving others. And she lived for the day, wholly present moment by moment.

Bill Gates

Bill Gates is another incredible leader. He started Microsoft with a dream years ago to create a computer that wasn't the size of a room, a personal computer that could sit on a desk. He enlisted the assistance of other people so that he could focus on that computer. He is arguably one of the most amazing computer gurus in the world, and that's what he excels at. So he could stay focused on what he does best, he brought in a business partner to be the driving force of the actual business at Microsoft. Bill Gates has always been an incredible philanthropist, not just now that he's one of the richest men in the world, but throughout his whole life. He's given back to every community he's lived in; he's always been of service to others. He is detail-oriented... living fully today... has this pull with people... The same qualities began to fall into place for me.

I looked at business leaders, and then I looked at some of my own friends – Juan Carlos Barrios, who taught me how to love people, and Michael Clouse, who taught me about recruiting and network marketing. I started to look at their qualities, and I saw the same fit. It was almost surreal. I went back to religion and politics, though, because I wanted to find out if there was a very specific leadership style and a roadmap that would fit any pendulum. I wanted to take any great leader in the world and see if I could fit them into the ten categories.

Warren Buffett

I've always had an admiration for Warren Buffett. Warren Buffett is the CEO of Berkshire Hathaway, a conglomerate holdings company. He also owns two network marketing companies. He's an absolutely amazing guy. Warren Buffett came from very humble beginnings, but he discovered a passion for investing, and he's always stayed true to that. Because he's never deviated from this, he has become one of the most amazing investors in the world. Investing is Warren Buffet's core task.

With Berkshire Hathaway, he stays focused on the actual investing. He hires CEOs and managers and surrounds them with people to fill in the gaps, which is an incredible strategy. Warren Buffett, like the other leaders I've studied, has a reason for what he does that's insurmountable – it's unstoppable, bigger than anything you could ever imagine.

Warren Buffett has an amazing ability to captivate people when he speaks and when he's around them. He's a man of few words, but when he speaks, people listen. He has an ability to get a point across that's second to none. This ability is due to the incredible trust and mentorship he's built into his life. It's worth noting that somebody as significant and successful as Warren Buffett openly gives credit to his mentors. He's also a very generous philanthropist. He doesn't have to share his investment information and prowess with competitors and governments around the world, but he does. And in his business, his service to others is impressive.

Steve Jobs

Steve Jobs, another incredible leader, started Apple computers. What a great story he has! In spite of his own personal adversities, he just keeps going forward. I found out that Steve, like all leaders at some point in their lives, came under incredible criticism and skepticism. He was really persecuted. At one point in time, the U.S. government even tried to put him in jail. Now, whether that's good or bad is not the point of the story; what's important is his incredible ability to stay focused and get the job done in spite of some incredible frustrations and rejections in his own life.

One of the things that gave me solace as I studied all these leaders is the fact that at some point in their lives every one of them was completely abandoned by most of the people around them, with the exception of a trusted few people that stuck with them through everything. This reminded me of my own journey, that first year in network marketing when most of the people in my life abandoned me, except for a few incredible people that stuck with me. I'm not comparing myself to these leaders, because I'm working on those forty things I've identified, but it is very reassuring for me to realize that they'd been through similar types of tribulations.

I guarantee that some of you reading this book right now are feeling the same way. You might be at a point in your life where you've been trying really hard, but you've been abandoned by everybody around you. I hope that my sharing this makes you realize that tomorrow is a new day, and there will be other people in your life. Some of the greatest leaders in the world have had to rebuild everything.

One of my best friends, somebody that I've been working with in my business for the last ten months, is Jim Kerr from Toronto, Canada. He's been in network marketing for a couple of years and is making very significant money. He did a training for me in my home, and during that training he gave me the gift of a phrase, something that exemplifies exactly what these leaders are made of. The phrase was, "Your why should make you cry."

In our business, we always tell people that they must be anchored to a reason for what they do, a reason so deep, so complex, that even on the worst days when they want to quit, this reason will keep them going. My childhood and my dad's death are my reasons. I found out that all leaders have their own deep reasons.

I became really intrigued as I saw complete similarities in absolutely opposite-end-of-the-spectrum types of leaders. Religion, politics, business… the same core qualities were present in every one of the leaders in each of these fields. There are lots of other leadership qualities, and others have written books on them. But I've narrowed it down to ten. I began asking myself, "Have I found a roadmap for myself?" I believed I had, but I wasn't finished yet.

I looked at other businesses, because I'm just enthralled with business. I've been an entrepreneur my whole life, as you learned in the first chapter. I have a disease. My wife laughs every time I say this, and in magazine interviews, I say straight out that my disease is called entrepreneurialism. I want to be a great business leader. I want to be remembered as a great business leader, but the right type of leader.

John F. Kennedy

One of my mentors shared with me his theory that there are really only two types of leaders in the world: dictators and heart-driven leaders. That mentor used John F. Kennedy as an example of a leader that leads from the heart. I began to do some research on John F. Kennedy. John F. Kennedy is an example of a heart-driven leader, while at the opposite end of the spectrum Adolf Hitler and other tyrants of the world epitomize true dictators. As I developed my own leadership skill, I wanted to be perceived as somebody like John F. Kennedy. He was loved and revered by millions of people; he had a very soft leadership style, which was evident in how he operated every day. He was probably one of the most caring leaders that America has ever known. He was an incredibly heart-led person. He had a real ability to attract people and make people love him. Kennedy had some really significant things happen in his childhood that drove him through the rest of his life. He was incredibly articulate, a powerful speaker, and he had an amazing ability to build trust in those around him.

Similarities between Gandhi and Kennedy

It's interesting to note that both Gandhi and John F. Kennedy were assassinated at very young ages. Both of them had similar leadership characteristics. Both of them had an incredible desire to follow a unique path, and both of them were completely focused on one thing in each of their lives. It was politics for Kennedy and liberation and religion for Gandhi. They each discovered what I call their "core task." Once they identified their driving force, their core task, they stuck to it. They never deviated from it, no matter what the cost. Both of them had this amazing "gravitational pull," which is a phrase I coined. When they walked into a room, other people noticed. They each had smiles that were captivating – people just seemed to want to be around them. People could feel their hearts; both of them had this amazing ability to communicate, both verbally and nonverbally.

Neither of them had ever taken specific training in communication, but they were great at saying what was on their mind or speaking in general. They knew how to use intonations. Both of them had this incredible ability to gain and give trust and loyalty. Both Gandhi and Kennedy were supremely confident, and both of them attributed much of their success to having mentors. I was amazed at how similar these two men were, even though they were worlds apart.

Even though they were from different periods of time and different sides of the world, both of them committed their entire lives to serving others. They both were very detail-oriented and able to balance lots of things in their lives at the same time. They were excellent multitaskers, and regardless of the pressures around them, they had the ability to stay present and live in the now.

I too aspired to be a really strong leader. I wanted to be somebody that could truly assist millions of people to achieve success. I began to realize that I had stumbled on a formula for the becoming the kind of leader I wanted to be.

Pierre Trudeau

Pierre Trudeau was one of Canada's greatest prime ministers. He reminds me a lot of John F. Kennedy. He was flamboyant. He always had a very *je ne sais quoi* attitude about him. He was extremely charismatic. That same gravitational pull existed in him. He had an incredible core task. Pierre Trudeau was instrumental in bringing the Canadian Charter of Rights and Freedoms into being. Canada was a British colony that became independent under the British North America Act. After many years, there was an uprising and a division in Canada. As prime minister, Trudeau was able to keep people together and move legislation through the House of Commons in Canada that led to the greatest law of Canada's history, the Canadian Charter of Rights and Freedoms. He was often highly criticized, but he led through love and created a high degree of trust.

After studying these seven world leaders, I was blown away by how much they had in common. I could not believe that in spite of being from different worlds, different walks of life, they possessed the same core values, the same personality traits. Through that simple gift from my wife a true roadmap for success had been revealed to me, and I want to share it with you! Over the past four years, I have focused on these ten traits, and through applying the traits to my life, I have been able to create incredible wealth and stronger relationships than I have ever had. Trust me, if you follow apply these ten traits to your life, "the sky's the limit!"

I found that all of these leaders stayed focused, identified their core task, and identified what brought them prosperity. Prosperity is a very significant word for me. Prosperity to religious leaders means something different than it means to business leaders and political leaders. All the leaders I've mentioned stayed absolutely core-focused (another phrase I've coined) on their core task.

Now, in our industry, an industry that I love to death, our core task is prospecting and introducing new people to our business. But in other businesses – for instance, in Warren Buffett's world – the core task is investing. In Bill Gates' world, the core task is computer programming. In John F. Kennedy's world, the core task was politics, and in Mother Teresa's, praise for her Lord. These leaders all stayed focused. They were all driven by incredible reasons for what they did. They all had this ability to pull people towards them, to communicate well, to build and give trust, to have confidence, to openly seek out and find mentors, and to give credit to those mentors. They remained humble and in service to others at all costs. This is a very important point. I noticed that all of them were constantly shot down and criticized by other people, and yet it was like water off a duck's back for them. They never let it get to them. And even to their biggest critics, they gave love back in return.

They were all detail-oriented and multitaskers, and they all had the ability to live in the now.

I started to see the ten traits in many incredible leaders....

Three Successful Business Entrepreneurs in America Today: Steven Scott, Greg Fullerton, and Fred Ninow

In my most recent business endeavor in network marketing, I have had the incredible opportunity to get to know three amazing men – three business success stories. Steve Scott, Greg Fullerton, and Fred Ninow come from three different types of business, but they have partnered on their latest endeavor. These three men have taught me so much about business and life. In getting to know them, I was able to easily identify the ten characteristics in them. This was amazing for me, as it told me that the ten traits provided a true roadmap, and reinforced for me that the world's greatest inspirational leaders had those qualities.

Steven K. Scott has had an awesome life so far. All of the leadership qualities I've mentioned are true of him. His core task is marketing. He built one of the largest direct response television companies in the world, American Telecast. He was fired from his first ten jobs. Everybody shunned him. Everybody cast him aside, everybody abandoned him, but he stuck with it, and finally in his eleventh business enterprise, he built a million-dollar company, then a second one, and then a third one. He has literally sold billions of dollars worth of products on TV. He still gets criticized many times by many people (criticisms that I believe are unfounded), but he always stays focused on his core task.

His *New York Times* best-selling book, *The Richest Man Who Ever Lived*, tells the story of King Solomon, the youngest king of Israel, and how he lived his life. If you never read another book, read this one. When Steve Scott was at the lowest point in his life, down-and-out and completely broke, one of his mentors suggested that he read the Book of Proverbs every day. There are thirty chapters in Proverbs and thirty days in a month. His mentor told him that if he read Proverbs every day for two years and implemented what he read, he would be successful beyond his wildest dreams for years to come. And that's exactly what happened. His book is all about the adversity he went through. It's a life-changing book. In spite of Steve Scott's billion dollars in revenue that he's created, he's just an average, humble person.

Greg Fullerton was one of the original founders of FranklinQuest, which eventually merged with Stephen Covey and became the billion-dollar company, FranklinCovey. Greg has a very caring heart. He knows what he's good at, and he never deviates from it. The stories that fill his life and that drive him are unbelievable. One of the stories that I remember Greg sharing that motivates him every day is that he and his wife had a child born prematurely at twenty-seven weeks gestation (talk about your why making you cry!). The baby fit into the palm of his hand, and I can see this so clearly in my mind. The baby's skin was translucent, like a baby bird's, and nobody expected this baby to survive.

Greg went each day to the hospital, and on three separate occasions the baby was pronounced dead. It was considered a medical miracle, the youngest child ever born in the University of Utah Hospital. When this little baby girl was born, the doctor gave him a brochure entitled, *When Hello Means Good-Bye*. Nobody expected this child to live, but today Carly is a vibrant young adult. This situation was the driving force behind what Greg Fullerton is today. Communication. Trust. Mentorship. Greg Fullerton is someone I aspire to be like today; he has had such a profound impact on me that the reason I will be more successful tomorrow than I am today will be largely because of Greg Fullerton.

Fred Ninow is a multimillionaire, and he is one of the most trusted people in my life today. He's the same type of leader. He knows what he's good at; he's a business expert. His reasons for what he does are inspiring. He's always been the type of person to just get out there and gets things done. He's a great communicator. Fred Ninow is not about making money, although he's made millions. He is the most family-first person I've ever met in my life. I've seen him walk away from business deals worth millions of dollars in order not to be late for his son's football game. He rarely travels because he wants to be around his kids. I spoke to him this morning about something very significant in our business, and he asked me if we could talk about it later because he was assisting his son to get new cleats. He highly values his wife Stacy and his children. He's an incredible inspiration to me.

Joel Osteen – Another Example

Joel Osteen is an incredible leader in the world today, someone who has the ear of both government heads and business heads. His why is unbelievable. His core task is being dedicated to spreading God's word in his life. And you know what? When he decides he wants to do something, he does it.

Here's an amazing story about Joel Osteen. Years ago, Joel and his father were building their congregation with Lakewood Church in Houston, Texas. They were in downtown Houston, and Joel had this idea. The Compaq Center, where the Houston Rockets basketball team played, was up for sale, and Joel had this vision to buy it and to turn it into a church.

So many people told him he was crazy and that it would never happen. Many people were telling him just to stay focused on the incredible congregation he had at the time, but he had this dream that was bigger than life, and he made it happen. Today the Compaq Center in downtown Houston *is* Lakewood Church. It's one of the largest congregations in America – 30,000 people walk through those doors every Sunday to listen to the words of the Lord that are shared by Joel Osteen and his associate pastor. This is an absolutely amazing story. And again, he openly credits his mentors. Joel Osteen's book, *Becoming a Better You*, is an unbelievable personal development book. It talks about all the qualities that I've been telling you about, and I found it to be a real roadmap for me. This is another must read.

Three Types of Leadership

What happened next was really exciting for me. I remembered those words from one of my mentors about there being two types of leaders (dictators and heartfelt leaders), and I thought about how I just never felt at peace with that. I didn't believe that there were just two types of leaders. I've always believed, and I mean this with my whole heart, *that we are all born leaders.* Think about this: When children are born, the mannerisms they develop, the way they talk, they way the act, all come from their parents. Parents are leaders. *Any ability for one human being to affect another human being is truly leadership.*

That's where I got the idea that there were actually ***three*** types of leaders. I believe that there are three types of leaders in the world, and WE ARE ALL leaders in one of three areas: **Authoritarian – Complacent – Inspirational.** In order to make this simpler to understand, I have broken down these three types in a later chapter and given you some easy-to-follow ideas so you can see exactly where you are. Once you have identified where you fit on the leadership continuum, then it is as easy as applying the ten traits to your life and watching yourself progress along the continuum.

The Seven Inspirational Leaders

1. Mahatma Gandhi

2. Mother Teresa

3. Bill Gates

4. Warren Buffett

5. Steve Jobs

6. John F. Kennedy

7. Pierre Trudeau

The Ten Core Traits of Inspirational Leaders

1. Have a mentor – be a mentor.

2. Be the best at your core task.

3. Have a why that makes you cry.

4. Be an excellent communicator.

5. Be supremely confident.

6. Be detail-oriented and learn to multitask.

7. Have a strong gravitational pull.

8. Serve others; inspire trust and loyalty.

9. Live in the present moment.

10. Be action driven.

The Value of Having a Roadmap

We all lead busy lives, and all of us are at different stages. Some of you may be feeling the pain of abandonment and rejection right now. Maybe you are tired of always trying to put your best foot forward. That's why I began studying leaders and isolating the traits they have in common. The goal is for all of us to achieve prosperity beyond our wildest dreams, with legions of friends and colleagues that trust us and love us. You can benefit from incredible mentors in your lives, and you can master network marketing in the process. Regardless of where you're at right now, what you have going on, or how big your own business is, once you determine where you are on the leadership continuum, if you apply the ten traits of these inspirational leaders to your life, you can obtain whatever level of prosperity you dream of, simply by switching your focus from the money to these ten traits. I know you can, because that is what I did.

In the coming chapters, you will learn where you fit onto the leadership continuum, what the ten traits really are and how to apply them to your life, what the secrets to success are, and what pitfalls to avoid along the way.

3

Three Types of Leaders

*"If I have seen farther than others,
it is because I was standing on the shoulder of giants."*
ISAAC NEWTON

W e are all born with leadership potential. In many people, that potential remains undeveloped. The real question to ask yourself is this: Do you want to be average, or do you want to be great? Do you want to be just okay, or do you want to be amazing? Do you want to be standard, or do you want to be exceptional? I see leadership as a continuum; at one end of the continuum, there is the biggest group of leaders, and at the other end of the pendulum, there are the leaders that I've profiled. I like to call the folks that I profiled "inspirational leaders" because they are inspirations to me.

We Are All Born Leaders

You might say, "I'm a follower; I'm not a leader." But here's something to think about. Have you ever known a father who was in the military and his son joined the military (like me)? Or how about a parent who isn't the most energetic person in the world, a parent who ends up on the couch every day after dinner? More often than not, if you take a look at complacency, complacency in a parent ends up being complacency in their children.

My wife is a great example of leadership. She is my true inspiration in life. She's down to earth; she's very humble. She's not materialistic. (Thank God she's not, because I love buying cars!) But material things just don't matter to her. She's so grounded it's incredible. And our children are becoming just like that. I now tend to focus on loving the simple things in life because my wife has taught me that the emotions I experience during simple situations are what is truly important. We go for walks, something I never used to do. We enjoy just being with our kids, and I'm seeing my children developing these same traits.

Then there are parents that are lethargic and don't want to go anywhere. They don't have good eating habits. There's a better than average chance that their children will end up the same way. That's an example of leadership. If your example influences another person to do the same thing, you're leading them. This is why I believe that everybody is born a leader.

The Leadership Continuum – Three Types of Leaders

As I began to study leadership, I discovered that there are three basic types of leaders, three basic leadership styles. Kurt Lewin, a psychologist, led a group of researchers in 1939 in a study designed to identify different styles of leadership. Over the years further research has uncovered more specific types of leadership, but this early study laid the groundwork, establishing three major leadership styles: laissez-faire, authoritarian, and democratic. As I continued to study, I refined the categories this way: *complacent, authoritarian,* and *inspirational.*

Complacent Leaders
This is the biggest category of leaders, made up of 90 percent of the people in the world. These are leaders who just meander through

life, nine-to-fivers, those who don't do any more than they have to. These are individuals that just sort of float along. You might not think they should be called leaders at all, but as I mentioned above, if others follow them and emulate their behavior, then they are leading others, albeit passively.

Authoritarian Leaders

Next there are authoritarian leaders. These are leaders who are very strong and aggressive. Their motto is "Do as I say, not as I do." An example of an authoritarian leader who has done incredibly well in life is Lee Iacocca of the Chrysler Corporation and author of *Where Have All the Leaders Gone?* He ruled with an iron fist. It was his way or the highway; he had a very authoritarian style. He has been quoted as saying that there is one word to describe a successful manager: decisiveness. He believed that you had to be able to think on your feet. He took risks and wasn't afraid of making unpopular decisions, with little or no feedback from his superiors, peers, or subordinates.

Really terrible authoritarian leaders are called dictators. Hitler was one of these, and Genghis Khan is another example. They are unrealistic in their demands, believe that all the decision-making power is theirs alone, and they do not allow others to question these decisions or their authority. These are the worst of the worst.

Authoritarian leadership is often appropriate in emergencies and extreme situations, but it tends to be disempowering and frustrating to those who must answer to this type of leader.

Inspirational Leaders

At the opposite end of the continuum are those leaders that are loved by everybody. They're not perfect. But these leaders embody the ten qualities of leadership, and their leadership comes from the heart. I call this leadership style inspirational leadership.

As Green Bay Packers' coach Vince Lombardi said, "Leadership is based on a spiritual quality; the power to inspire, the power to inspire others to follow."

John F. Kennedy exhibited this type of leadership style. He had a keen understanding of people that was warm and affectionate, yet calculating at the same time. He respected those who worked for him and with him, but he was also quick to assess where each individual would fit best and be the most effective. He was a great communicator, and made it easy for others to communicate with him. Kennedy's speeches are some of the most inspiring of any politician, past or present. John F. Kennedy had a special ability to energize those he led.

AUTHORITARIAN   COMPLACENT   INSPIRATIONAL

Dictator   Ego-Driven   Demanding   Procrastinator   Indecisive   Excuses   Caring   Connector   Heartfelt   Inspirational

The Ten Core Traits of Inspirational Leaders

As I studied each of the seven world leaders that I mentioned in Chapter Two, I saw that they each possessed these ten traits. It was amazing to me because they came from three uniquely different walks of life. When I started to look at the leaders in my own life that I admired, I saw the traits almost like musical notes jumping off the sheet. I knew that if I started to apply these ten traits, I couldn't help but be a better person, and I would start to achieve the success I was looking for in life. My heartfelt belief is that if YOU apply these ten traits to your life, you too can achieve whatever level of prosperity you desire.

1. Have a mentor – be a mentor.

Don't reinvent the wheel; seek out coaches and mentors who are where you want to be, and be open and humble enough to listen to them and do what they say. Make sure you choose trustworthy mentors – use the material in this chapter to assist you. When you achieve success, others will seek you out for mentorship, and you'll be able to provide them with a proven path to their goals and dreams.

2. Be the best at your core task.

All the leaders I studied had a single focus that carried them from the early days of their enterprises into their successful futures. In network marketing, your core task is prospecting. This is your main focus, and like all top leaders, you don't want to deviate from it. Develop your skills, become a master prospector, and watch your business soar!

3. Have a why that makes you cry.

Even after all these years, my why can still move me to tears. It doesn't matter that I've reached many of my goals – thinking about my own experiences as a child continue to motivate me to create a very different life for my children, no matter what! Your why should have this same intensity; if it doesn't, then dig deeper to come up with one that does.

4. Be an excellent communicator.

Leaders communicate. In your own endeavor, becoming a skilled communicator is essential. Ours is a business of connecting with people, and no matter what your personality type, you can learn to create rapport and interact with others. Words are powerful – learn to use them effectively.

5. Be supremely confident.

All the leaders I studied had a high degree of self-confidence. They each encountered many obstacles and lots of rejection along the way, but they didn't let this affect their morale. Each in their own way was bold, courageous, unflappable, full of determination and tenacity. Your path to the top will require this as well.

6. Be detail-oriented and learn to multitask.

One trait of all great leaders is the ability to be organized, pay attention to details, and multitask. Life is full of interruptions, and the urgent will always be louder than the truly important. On your path to leadership, make sure you have a system in place that supports your focus and drives you forward.

7. Have a strong gravitational pull.

Leaders in every field have an incredible ability to pull people towards them; people are just naturally drawn to them. This comes from being congruent and living from the inside out – as well as having a deep sense of compassion for others. The more you connect with your own unique calling and abilities, the more others will just naturally be drawn to you too.

8. Serve others; inspire trust and loyalty.

Trustworthy leaders inspire others to trust them; they have many loyal followers. This is not because they exert control or power over others – it's because they have chosen to serve others. This type of leader has learned to leave his or her ego at the door and put others first.

9. Live in the present moment.

All leaders are visionary, but they aren't so future-driven that they can't fully enjoy the present moment. On the contrary, they experience the present in its fullness. When you are with one of these leaders, you sense that they are living in the now, even while they are working to achieve future goals. On your own journey, make sure you experience each and every day to the max.

10. Be action driven.

Achieving your goals involves knowing what you want and then taking the necessary action to make success happen. Be a "do it now" kind of person – learn from the examples of the powerful leaders I studied, and create the success you dream of.

Your Own Leadership Style

Regardless of where you are on the continuum, you can begin to focus on your own journey toward inspirational leadership. Understanding the three types of leaders and the ten core traits of the inspirational leaders you want to model provides the roadmap to success that you can easily follow.

4

Finding a Great Mentor

"I was lucky to have the right heroes. Tell me who your heroes are and I'll tell you how you'll turn out to be. The qualities of the one you admire are the traits that you, with a little practice, can make your own, and that, if practiced, will become habit-forming."
WARREN BUFFETT

If you are really serious about being successful, *find a good mentor*. It's not necessarily the biggest income earner in your company, either. Find somebody who is successful, but make sure that individual has the same ethical principles and morals as you do. Don't be afraid to interview a few people before you choose somebody to follow, and until you're making a huge paycheck, don't be afraid to be a bit of a follower. *Be coachable.* When you have big goals, it's much easier to walk in the footsteps of others than to create your own path.

Picture a northern Canadian morning. You look out your window and see four feet of fresh snow outside. Imagine trying to walk through that snow all by yourself – you're up to your knees in it, trudging along. As you pull your feet out of the snow, one slow step at a time, your boot nearly comes off. Now think about how much easier it would be if somebody else has already walked where you want to go, and all you have to do is step into their footprints every step of the way. How much easier would it be to get where you want to go? This is exactly what our business is about. If you want to build it big, follow somebody else's footsteps. Never stop learning, and always stay coachable.

Warren Buffett's Mentor

Warren Buffett, the world's greatest investor and one of the leaders I studied, credits much of his success to his mentors. When he began his career, he was mentored by an Englishman named Benjamin Graham, who is often referred to as the dean of financial analysis. Graham was born in London in 1894 and moved to New York City with his parents when he was still an infant. He graduated from Columbia University with his BS at age twenty and started his financial career as a messenger for a Wall Street firm. He worked his way up through the company, eventually becoming a full partner. Graham was earning $600,000 a year by the time he was twenty-five years old – and this was in 1919! That's literally millions in today's dollars. Although his firm survived the stock market crash in 1929, Graham lost all of his personal fortune. He became determined to recreate his fortune and teach others to do the same. His goal became teaching investors how to build wealth in a conservative and rational manner. He taught that investing is a discipline – one that takes research, training, and experience.

Warren Buffett absorbed Ben Graham's simple yet profound investment principles at the age of twenty-one, and he became captivated by this financial expert. Buffett discovered that his mentor was the chairman of a small, unknown insurance company named GEICO. He took a train to Washington D.C. one Saturday morning to find the headquarters. When he got there, the doors were locked. Unstoppable, Buffett began pounding on the door until a janitor opened it for him. He asked if there was anyone in the building. There was – Loren Davidson, the vice president of finance, was working on the sixth floor. The two men met, and Buffett began questioning him about the company and its business practices. This conversation lasted for four hours. This led to Buffett meeting and being mentored by Ben Graham, an experience that stayed with Buffett for the rest of his life. Eventually he acquired the entire GEICO company through his corporation, Berkshire Hathaway. He never fails to acknowledge what he learned from Graham.

Early Mentors

I've always known the value of having a mentor. When I was on the SWAT team, we always had a team leader; he was the most senior guy on the SWAT team. Being on a SWAT team is dangerous at all times, and one bad decision could cost someone's life – my own or one of my partner's. We worked as a unified team, but we always followed the directions of the team leader; we always trusted his advice. We followed that advice explicitly, because doing so could mean the difference between life and death.

For instance, I learned from my SWAT team leader how to enter a building. Following his lead, when we went into a building I would veer off to the left, clear a room, and wait there. Even though my instincts might have told me *not* to wait there, by opening the next door too soon I could throw off the entire plan, and somebody could get hurt; I could kill myself or end up being killed in the process.

I learned to follow the advice of that leader to the letter, even if my own instincts told me something different. I managed to stay alive and unhurt throughout my SWAT team experience, and so did everyone else on our team. We always achieved every outcome we envisioned – whether it was freeing hostages or boarding ships or raiding drug houses. Knowing that people with guns and knives were on the other sides of those doors, following the advice and direction of my team leader and acting on his experience was crucial. It was this ability to act on somebody else's experience with complete trust that kept me alive. The lessons I learned on the SWAT team have guided me through the rest of my life.

My first real experience having a business mentor was when I opened my mortgage company back in 2001. I didn't know much about the mortgage industry, but I knew of some very successful mortgage brokers in Ottawa where I was living. Being the brazen person I am, I called up the top mortgage broker in Ottawa, because I was determined to build a huge mortgage business and make a fortune. I wanted to make more money than this top broker did. I told him straight out, "I want to learn everything I can about mortgages. I've always gone right to the top in anything I've done."

His response? He laughed hysterically at me over the phone. I'll never forget that. Of course, I asked the only logical question anyone would ask when somebody laughs at you for asking an honest question: "Why are you laughing?"

His answer was very simple. "Kid, why the heck would I ever train my competition?"

He continued, "You've got to be out to lunch! You really ought to just quit while you're ahead. You're just going to hurt yourself."

I said, "Why do you say that?"

He said, "Beause *you're* coming to *me* looking for advice. Kid, fish shouldn't swim with sharks."

I laughed right back at him, and I retorted with another question. "Hey, listen, what if I pay you?"

He said, "What are you talking about?"

Finding a Great Mentor

I said, "I'll give you $10,000 for just one day if you'll promise to tell me honestly every single thing I need to do to be successful in the mortgage industry."

He laughed again, but he agreed. I don't know to this day why he agreed, because that wasn't a lot of money for him, but we spent one very incredible day together. He literally opened up to me, telling me everything he knew about mortgages. In turn, I applied every bit of that advice.

He encouraged me to focus on relationships. He told me that if I wanted create a significant business in the mortgage industry, then I should build relationships with real estate agents and other referral sources and not worry about individual mortgages. He taught me that if I treated those people honestly and ethically and built friendships with them, they would provide me with the mortgages I was seeking to arrange.

He also told me to be very accurate with my paperwork. Now, I hated paperwork, but because of that advice I learned to keep accurate notes and records. I learned to pick just a couple of key lenders to work with and refer all my business to. He advised me to get to know the loan officers and become familiar with the conditions those banks offered. Following his advice, I became an expert in these areas.

I did everything he told me, and I started to make just as much money as he did. Two years later, because of this mentor I was earning over a million dollars a year, and I was able to build my mortgage business part-time while I was still a homicide detective. I had nine full-time employees, and we funded hundreds of millions of dollars in mortgages.

What was ironic about this whole experience is that I did become that mentor's competitor, but he never looked at it that way. We became great friends, and he began coaching me on real estate investments and other areas related to the mortgage industry. I still have a relationship with him to this day. I don't deal with him as much now, but it's important for you to know that the mentors you have at one stage in your life probably will not be your mentors for your entire life. You'll go in different directions, you'll follow different roads, and you'll acquire new mentors along the way.

Here in Toronto where I live now, there's an incredible entrepreneur that I have a lot of respect for. His name is Derek Baird. Derek owns several real estate practices; he's built offices from the ground up. He's a real estate investor, and he's made millions and millions of dollars for himself. He's written books on mentorship, and currently he mentors many people.

As I developed a friendship with him, we talked many times about the subject of mentorship and how important it was. He gives credit to his mentors for all of his success, which is amazing because he has been such an inspiration me. One of the things he taught me is that when you choose a mentor, the relationship with that mentor should serve both of you. What he means is that when you're looking for a mentor, obviously you're seeking advice to assist you to be more successful or prosperous, but your mentor also requires something out of that relationship.

This has served me in many ways. In my experience, I've had mentors that I thought had pure intentions. I thought they just wanted to assist me, but I found out afterwards that they were using me for their own good, and I discovered that they lied to me in the process. They definitely had something in it for themselves, although they told me they didn't. I've had other mentors who told me right up front what was in it for them.

If you're looking for a mentor, make sure that it's a win/win situation for both you and your mentor. Otherwise, neither of you will receive the full potential from that mentorship.

Be Careful Who You Choose as Your Mentor

My experience with mentorship in network marketing began during my first couple of months in the business. As I started to do well, a millionaire in my upline offered to coach me. I was blinded by his success, so I began following his lead without ever questioning him. He told me that if I wanted to make a million dollars in network marketing, I had to do *exactly* what he told me and *never* doubt him.

I was so enthralled by network marketing and with the potential to make millions in residual income that I followed him without questions. Little did I know that he was a tyrant, one of the worst dictators I've ever encountered. I never saw it. He advised me to forget about people, that success was all about business volume. He coached me to build my business knowing that there would always be people that would let me down.

People in my organization would come to me with frustrations, and he would tell me to just forget about them. I remember him saying, "Forget about that person. They're just going to drag you down. There's no potential to that person." I wanted so badly to be successful that I just followed his lead.

He also used to dangle gifts in front of me all the time. He'd buy me lunch, or he'd buy me a new suit or tie. He was always reminding me of all the things he did for me and all the reasons I should be loyal to him. He made an example of me to others in such an arrogant way that people started to hate me. I hung out with him so much that I developed the same personality traits as him.

As I mentioned in the first chapter, by the end of my first year in network marketing some very important people in my life abandoned me because they told me I was becoming too much like that mentor; they told me I was becoming a dictator. Finally, I saw it. It was a very painful experience, but at least now I had an example of what I didn't want to be like as a leader and as a mentor, and I immediately broke away from this man.

The Right Kind of Mentor

Not long after this experience, another mentor came in my life who assisted me with releasing the emotions I had created after being so influenced by my previous mentor. This individual really opened my eyes to leadership. He taught me that there are two types of leaders.

He said, "There are dictators, and you know who they are. Your old mentor was one. The worst dictator was obviously Adolf Hitler. He murdered millions of people who didn't conform to his ways; he is the most extreme example of dictatorship."

While Hitler and others like him (i.e., Genghis Kahn) are the extreme, there are other authoritarian leaders who lead with an iron fist. Their philosophy is "Do as I say and not as I do," belittling and berating people in the process.

He went on to say, "There are also incredible leaders like John F. Kennedy who rule through love. Kennedy ruled with respect, and he won the hearts of millions of people in the process. Ken, you have a choice. You can either be a dictator, or you can rule through love and respect and trust."

This mentor shared much wisdom and advice with me over the next couple of years, and he led me in a direction that really assisted me to become who I am and to earn the income that I earn today. But guess what? Once again I became blinded to a mentor. I never knew what he was really after, even though one of the things I found very peculiar was that when we first started to work together he demanded to be my only mentor. He also said that if I was ever in any other business, he would require that I give him the option to be above me in that business. In return for his years of wisdom, I had to agree to this and never challenge it. Because he gave me such great advice about defining leadership, I agreed. It worked well for a while, but eventually I discovered the reality of who he was. I found out that he had lied about some of the things in his past.

He became very aggressive with me, demanding that I stick to my commitment to him, but I realized in my heart that he had his own motives that were incongruent with mine, and I became aware that he was using me. Behind the scenes he was doing unethical things to try and make as much money as he could, and it became evident that he didn't really care about people, so I broke away from him.

This was a very painful experience, because I owe part of my success today to this mentor. In spite of that, I couldn't be loyal to him because his heart wasn't in the right place. I saw that he was just out for himself, and fortunately I chose to walk away from him.

While I learned a lot from these two mentors and I respect them for that, at the same time they were tyrants with vile ulterior motives and I just couldn't continue to be mentored by either of them.

Coming out of my experience with that second mentor, although Derek Baird never knew about it, he gave me just the right advice at that time. He told me, "There's got to be something in it for both the mentor and the student. If somebody's telling you there isn't, don't mentor with that person. Be very suspicious of them."

Beware of the person who demands that! No one mentor knows everything. If you're choosing a mentor, make sure that there's something in it for both of you. Always find mentors that have the success you're looking for in the field you're looking in.

When you're with a mentor, always be very respectful of that mentor's time. If you ask your mentor for advice and then don't take it, then shame on you. That mentor has every right to not to want to mentor you anymore if you're wasting their time, because that person is already extremely busy.

Ideally, you should have several mentors in your life, depending on the areas you're seeking mentorship. I personally take advice from several mentors who are not involved in network marketing, and I still get advice from my original mentor, the mortgage broker, on real estate transactions.

Continually ask yourself what your core beliefs and values are. Be clear about what you believe in the most. Ask yourself, "Is the advice I'm getting from my mentor congruent with my own beliefs?" If the answer is no, then don't follow it. Stay true to yourself.

Another important thing is to openly give credit to your mentors. Don't ever take the credit. Don't feel that *you* have to be the source of the advice. As you progress, your advice will be a lot more valid to others if they hear the story of how you got that advice, so freely share it. If you're mentoring somebody, make sure that you're not afraid to give credit where credit is due.

When you find great mentors and begin to take advice from them, you'll become successful, and other people will start coming to you for advice. Be very careful to not get into this mode too quickly. Don't start offering advice to people unless you've truly succeeded at the level where you feel confident that your advice can be taken the right way. There are way too many teachers out there today who have never experienced what they teach.

Particularly in the network marketing industry, I see so many people giving advice to others – generic trainers and speakers who have never been successful themselves in a network marketing company. Be wary about taking advice from these people and trusting them as mentors. The saying, "Unless you've walked a mile in somebody's shoes…" should ring in your ears right now. Make sure that the mentor you're looking for has actually walked down the road you're seeking to travel. This is very, very important.

As you start to become successful, you'll become known in your business, but don't become a mentor to others until you're truly achieving the success that you want. I can't tell you the amount of experiences I've been through where I've observed people giving advice to others when they haven't been successful themselves yet.

When you become a mentor (and you will), don't be afraid to coach somebody else, but don't sacrifice yourself in the process. Remain a student yourself at all times. Continue to search for a better understanding, and you'll continually expand your mentorship. Today I coach many, many people about network marketing. I understand why – my family is earning several million dollars a year in direct sales.

Through my own experience, I've learned it's important to tell a lot of stories. Don't simply give advice based on what you think is accurate. Look back through your own experiences, and if you have an experience related to the advice you're giving, share that experience, and let your students come up with ideas or decisions based on the stories you tell. Looking back at all the mentors I've had, the greatest advice wasn't just the thoughts they verbalized; it was the stories they told about their own experiences. They always gave the credit to their mentors. I try to do the same thing every day, and you'll want to do this too. Another quality of a great mentor is that they always remain receptive to receiving mentorship. You'll never hear a great mentor say, "I know that already."

Always be the most passionate, the most incredible, the most loving, the most giving person in your organization. Don't worry about what people above you, below you, or beside you are doing. Work your business with your heart, be passionate about it, and give it an honest effort. Never worry about the people around you and what they're doing. Always stay focused on inviting new people to your business, because that's what we do – we're professional inviters. Be passionate about your business. Love the people that you're involved with!

Look at anybody that's earning a significant income in network marketing today. They all have the ability to deliver a message. They may not be the best speakers in the world, but they all communicate clearly. If you're not naturally a great speaker, take a public speaking course like Toastmasters. If you don't know enough about your company's products, learn more about them. If you require some tips about dressing well, talk to somebody who dresses well and ask him or her to assist you in choosing some new clothes.

Always try and improve yourself. Every day of the week, do something to better yourself. There are many ways to do this. Read books, watch videos, go to personal development conferences – make it your goal to improve every day. Not only will you reach more success than you've ever dreamed possible, you'll be able to be the kind of trustworthy mentor that paves the way for many others.

Tips to Finding the Right Mentors

* Be open to having several mentors.
* Understand what's in the relationship for both you and your mentor; make sure it's a win/win situation.
* Ask yourself if their beliefs and philosophy are congruent with your own ideals.
* Pick a mentor that can coach through personal stories.
* Choose a mentor that has mentors of his or her own.
* Make sure the mentor has walked down the path you are seeking to travel.
* Look for a mentor who is completely honest and ethical.

How to Steer Clear of the Wrong Mentors

* Be careful of mentors who make undue demands on you (unquestioning loyalty, for example).
* Don't get involved with mentors who are overly aggressive and controlling in their interactions with you.
* Be wary of any mentor whom you suspect of unethical business practices of any kind.
* Stay away from mentors who don't truly care about others.
* Never choose a mentor who you feel is dishonest about his past.
* Don't listen to a mentor who insists that you never question them.

5

Prospecting: Your Core Task

"Smart, committed people with the right support and vision can have a huge impact."
BILL GATES

Leaders in every area of life have one significant common thread: they identified their core task early on, and they stayed laser-focused on it. For the religious leaders I studied, their core task was love for God and service to others, period. They were presented with many other opportunities during the course of their lives, and they could have gone in other directions, but instead they never deviated from this core calling.

The greatest business leaders in the world also have identified what they're the best at and stayed completely focused on this, even though they may be involved in other businesses or projects. For example, Bill Gates might invest in other companies, but his core task as he identified it in early adulthood is designing computers, and he has never deviated from it. As a young boy, he excelled in science and mathematics. His parents recognized his gifts and enrolled him in a private school known for its demanding academic environment. When he was thirteen he got hooked on computers and surpassed the knowledge of his teacher within a week. Soon he wrote his first computer program. This was the start, and he has not deviated from his core focus since then. His core task is what brought him prosperity.

Prosperity as I define it transcends the types of leaders or the kinds of endeavors they are involved in. Prosperity for a religious leader is how close he or she is to God, how much he or she serves their Lord. That's what makes them prosper. Political leaders define prosperity as being significant and having an impact on issues that affect society. Prosperity for business leaders is not merely financial gain; they are driven by a desire for a greater good.

Our core task in network marketing is prospecting. Prospecting is the only thing you get paid for. Therefore, if you want to achieve prosperity in network marketing, it requires that you focus all your energy on prospecting, without distraction. Anything else will slow your progress in reaching your goals. And if your why is strong enough, it will propel you to accomplish what drives you.

Three Key Reasons

When I first got involved in network marketing, prospecting was easy for me. I'd call up a friend and say, "Hey, listen, I got involved in a new business. I want you to take a look at it." Most of the time, they wouldn't even look at it; they'd just give me their credit card. Now I realize that this was not duplicatible, but it did have something to do with credibility, and in all aspects of recruiting, this is paramount.

Beyond all the training I received about various systems or how to handle objections, the best advice I ever received was from Michael Clouse during a seminar I attended shortly after I began my network marketing career. He said, "People join this business for three reasons: They know you, they like you, and they trust you."

Trust is key. You might know someone, and you may like that person, but do you trust that individual? It's possible to be in business with somebody and trust him or her completely, even if you don't necessarily like them all that much. On the other hand, you may know and like someone, but when it comes to business, you absolutely do not trust them. There's no way you would ever want to be in business with them. Trust is key.

Relationship Building

What drives me today is my love of introducing new people to this business. It's all about relationship building, which involves a step-by-step process. Have you ever had the experience of striking up a conversation with someone at a party with the intent of prospecting them? You eventually hit them with that age-old, traditional introduction line: "Hey, you'd be good in my business," and you follow it with a myriad of statements about how great your product and opportunity is. The person seems interested, so you ask for their phone number, and they give it to you. You think the interaction went great, but when you call them back a few days later, they don't answer the phone.

A key distinction here is that your ability to prospect is tied to building relationships, not offending people. Often when you offend someone, they won't let on that they are offended. When you prospect someone at a party, while they might placate you by listening to what you have to say, the bottom line is that they might be a little bit offended that you'd bring up business at a party. They'll give you their phone number, but they have no intention of picking up the phone if you call.

Three Simple Steps

Since most of your time should be spent prospecting, you want to do it as efficiently as possible. Ninety percent of the network marketing businesses that I've built, I've built on the phone. I've worked from home. Would you rather be driving around from appointment to appointment, eating up hours, spending money on gas, or would you rather be sitting at home working the phone?

Regardless of whom I'm speaking to, whether they're a top leader in network marketing, somebody brand new to the business, or a local business leader, I always follow the exact same three steps – every single time.

These three steps are:

1. Call Them

2. Refer Them

3. Follow Up with Them

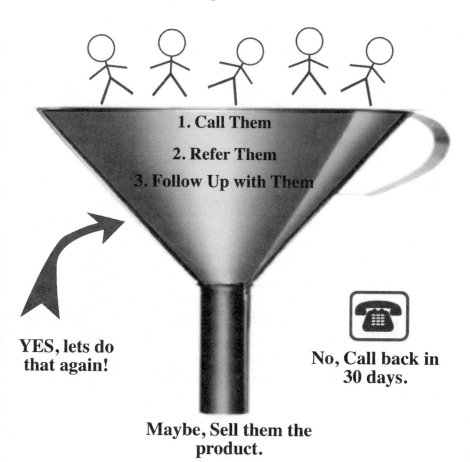

Imagine that you are pouring each of the prospects on your list into a funnel. Inside the funnel you go through three steps that allow your prospect to systematically review the merits of your opportunity, the owners, the management team, the product you're marketing, the compensation plan, and the timing of your company. At the other end of this systematic review, the prospect emerges as either a yes, a no, or a maybe. If you do it properly, and always focus on the relationship first, you'll produce incredible results.

Prospecting Is a Process

Prospecting is a process, not an event. I recently sponsored a woman in my network marketing business that I had been prospecting for three and a half years. When I first contacted her from an Internet ad, it wasn't the right time in her life. I stayed in touch with her regularly, and finally the time was right for her to join my team. *Prospecting is a process, not an event.* Many people get on the phone, and when prospects say no, they get frustrated and quit. But I've learned that a lot of the top prospectors in our business never try to finish the deal on the first call. Sometimes it takes years to get somebody into your business.

Build Friends, Not Income

I don't build income; I build friends. One of my mentors told me that a millionaire in network marketing is defined as someone who has a million friends. If you focus on relationships, the money truly does come later.

Many people choose not to join a network marketing business because they are offended at some point in the process. It might not be because they don't like the business, although they say that's their reason. If you can build trust in your prospects, the whole process is much easier.

One of the easiest ways to offend somebody is to prematurely bring up your business when they are not in a receptive mindset. I *never* begin the prospecting process unless it's a telephone call that I initiate. This enables me to steer clear of any pitfalls. For instance, at a party people are there to enjoy themselves; they are not there to look for a business opportunity.

The Law of Reciprocity

Reciprocity is the give and take of life. It's doing something for somebody else that they will feel indebted to repay. Let's say you're moving next Saturday. You call me and ask me to assist you, and of course (reluctantly) I agree because we're friends even though I hate moving. A few months later, I have to move. Who do you think I'm going to call first? You! And even though it's an inconvenience, you're going do assist me. Why? Because I assisted you. That's reciprocity.

Simple salutations are another example of reciprocity. I see you on the street, I walk up to you, and I say, "Hi, how are you doing today?" Of course, you reply right away, "Great, how are you doing?" Reciprocity is around us everywhere.

In the recruiting process, even though I never mention my opportunity the first time I meet anyone, I've developed a strategy I learned from my mentors. If I focus on getting to know someone first – if I begin to like them and trust them, and if they begin to like and trust me – then, by using the law of reciprocity, I can get their phone number every single time. My goal in any initial interaction with anyone is to start building a friendship and to obtain a phone number. That's it. If I think they might be a good fit in my business, that's all I'll do. I will not mention my product or my service intentionally.

Something else I never do is to hand out business cards. I don't even carry them. I use business cards for people in my downline, upline, or crossline that I want to keep in touch with. With my prospects, I only request business cards; I never give them.

There's one common subject that we all like to talk about that brings us incredible joy: ourselves. I engage my prospects in casual conversation, asking them lots of open-ended questions, and this leads them to willingly give me their phone numbers every time. Let's say I'm introduced to you at a social function. I think, "Wow, this person has a great personality. She'd be perfect for my business." Instead of bringing up my opportunity, I'll ask you about your family, your occupation, your hobbies. I'll pay very close attention to what you're saying, and I won't interrupt you.

Eventually I'm going to get you talking about something you really like, and then at that point, I'll stop the conversation, simply ask you for your phone number, and you'll give it to me. I'll say, "I've really appreciated talking to you. I've got to move on right now, but hey, can I have your phone number? I'd really like to call you back and hear more about your horses. They sound amazing." You'll be happy to give me your phone number. You'll think, "Wow, I really like Ken. He let me talk about myself and that brings joy to me, so I want to talk to him some more." Because I'm not actually mentioning business at that point, I'm still prospecting. I collect those phone numbers, and then I just pour those people back into the funnel.

What Are the Odds?

What are the odds of somebody you prospect joining your downline? One in ten, two in twenty, one in fifty, one in a hundred? Here is my theory: The odds of getting somebody to join a network marketing business are one in 365. Every person out there that you will ever talk to will join your business – even the most skeptical, negative person –if you get them on the right day. To me, that's the fun part, the exciting part, of prospecting.

People join a network marketing business for many reasons. One person joins because he wants to make more money. Someone else joins because she loves the product. Some folks join because they are looking for something new in their lives. Maybe they're sick and tired of being sick and tired. They're frustrated with their jobs. One person's reason might not necessarily be the money; it might be that he or she wants a challenge. Maybe an individual is having trouble at home, and this will provide something positive to focus on. For others, it's all the negative friends they have – they see all the positive people in network marketing and they want to be around them.

That's why prospecting is a process versus an event. If you agree with my theory that every single person will join, then it becomes just as important to develop a system for following up properly with people as it is to introduce this business initially to new people. Both parts of the equation are equally important. Without introducing new people regularly, you won't have anyone to follow up with. Without follow-up, no one will join.

A Game of Chance

Several months ago I was asked to speak at a major event at the Grand Hotel in Kelowna, British Columbia. During the day we had an amazing event with hundreds of people in attendance, and in the evening I visited the hotel casino.

I love people watching. I meandered up to a roulette table, where a group of fifteen people were gathered. Now, for those of you who aren't familiar with roulette, the game is played with a ball and a wheel. On the wheel there are thirty-eight spaces where the ball can stop – some are red and some are black, and they're divided equally around the wheel. There are two spots that are green; one is labeled zero, and the other one is double zero. Those playing the game bet on which color and specific numbers the ball will land on. The dealer spins the wheel, and then takes a little silver ball and spins it the opposite way. As the wheel slows down and the momentum of the ball decreases, the ball drops down into the inner wheel, bounces around crazily between the numbers, and then finally rests in one spot – and that's the winner.

I stayed at the roulette table for quite some time, watching the dealer motionlessly spinning that ball, over and over again. The ball would stop; he'd start again. The ball would stop again, and he'd start again. And then it hit me – I saw a parallel to prospecting. Let's say that the silver ball is your prospect, and the green zero is the moment they say yes. Think about this. It doesn't matter how often you speak to them – you want to speak to them in a way that allows you to spin the ball again. Once you've got somebody into the "like" stage, call them once a month.... Imagine that the ball is the person, the green zero is a yes, and there's a whole month on that wheel.

If the dealer keeps spinning that ball again, over and over and over, eventually that silver ball will land on the green zero. Eventually the prospect will say yes. You just never know when. It's the odds of the game – prospecting is a game of chance. Everybody will join a network marketing business, but you don't know when. You just have to keep spinning the ball... you just have to keep contacting them. You want to create a system, just like the dealer spinning that ball again and again.

Increase Your Odds

In the game of roulette, if there's one silver ball and forty places for it to stop, how do you get it to stop on the green zero more often? You're probably thinking, "Spin it more often." I want you to change that mindset. The real answer is: "Add more balls." Imagine that there are forty-two silver balls. Every time you spin the wheel, what happens? A prospect would join every single time the balls stopped. Wouldn't that be much easier?

Prospecting is very much like this. Someone is going to say yes every time. Remember, your chances of getting somebody to join are one in 365. The question is: Do you have the fortitude to stick with it? I did – I learned early on that if I just kept talking to people, focusing on getting to know them, like them, and trust them and vice versa, the rest would happen on its own. Just like the game of roulette, I learned to develop a system that would allow me to keep spinning the ball every day.

Your Master List

My system starts with a master list. I created my master list on day one in the business, and I do it again once a year. I write down every single person I meet. If this book has caused you to reexamine your methods for working your business and you want to reach for more, then remember that every day can be a new day in network marketing. Once you've finished reading this, make it day one in network marketing. Don't wait for the end of the book. Read about prospecting and defining your core task, and get to work.

Create a list of each of every person you've ever met in your life. This might sound corny to you; it sounded corny to me when someone, who happened to be a millionaire, first told me to do this. I didn't understand the importance of it at first, but after a couple of months when I started to get frustrated because things weren't working for me, I decided to write that list.

In the beginning, I just called my friends and said, "Hey, Joe, I just got started with this brand-new business; we're going to make a ton of money. The buy-in is $2,400. Give me your credit card." While I did have some initial success in getting people to join my business, after a couple of months my income wasn't going up, and some of my initial reps became frustrated and quit. That's when I realized how important systems were. I realized that how *you* prospect somebody is how you're training *your prospect* to prospect somebody. How *you* sponsor somebody into this business is the way *they'll* sponsor someone. I might be able to sign someone up by just asking for his credit card, but the average person can't do that.

Success in network marketing requires following a simple system from day one. Creating your master list is the first step. Begin by writing down every person you've ever met in your life. Get out your old high school yearbooks; don't worry about phone numbers at this point. Use the phone book as a memory jogger. The average person over the age of twenty has met more than 2,000 people, so your list should consist of hundreds of people.

Once you've compiled your master list, make another list of fifty or sixty people that have similar desirable characteristics. You are looking for the qualities that top income earners in network marketing all seem to share. You are creating your "dream team."

The Qualities of Top Income Earners

- They are hard workers.
- They are honest.
- They smile easily.
- They are positive and upbeat.

- They have incredible drive and motivation.
- They stand out in a crowd.

Select people from your master list as if you were putting together an NBA finals basketball team or a Stanley Cup-winning hockey team. These are the people you want to start with.

Now, begin putting this group of people through the funnel. Step one is initiating a phone call. Give them a call to rekindle or revitalize your relationship. My phone calls sound like this: "Hey, Dan, I'm just giving you a call because I was thinking about you. I got involved in a new business that I want to share with you. How are you doing today?" I introduce the reason I'm calling them, and then I change the subject as quickly as possible back to... them! Remember, we all enjoy talking about ourselves. I get them chatting about what's going on, and I make it fun and light. I always remember to smile when I'm on the phone – it really makes a difference.

During this initial conversation, never interrupt them in the middle of a sentence, no matter what. Engage their heart by asking them questions and letting them talk about things that matter to them. This is such an easy philosophy to follow on the phone. Your conversation might last ten or fifteen minutes, and then at some point there's a pause. This means the other person is satisfied. Now you can say, "Hey, listen, John. I really have to tell you about this business. It's amazing. I'd really like your opinion on it. Can you take a look at something for me?" This is where reciprocity kicks in. When they say, "Yes, of course," you can send them to your company's Web site, and then you can book an appointment to follow up with them.

If they're in your local area, you can say, "John, I want to get together and go over this with you after you've looked at the Web site. When do you have time for a coffee in the next couple of days?" John will agree because you've used reciprocity. Get a date booked right there on that first call. If it's a long-distance situation, you can say, "I want to call you back in a couple days. I'm available Thursday through Saturday between 5:00 and 8:00. Just give me a time that works for you." And then remember to be prompt and punctual when you do call them back.

Ninety percent of the call was about the prospect. You directed them to a Web site, and you booked an appointment. You didn't mention your product, or the compensation plan, or the owners of the company; instead, you focused on them, and you pointed them to a presentation. As one of my mentors taught me, "In network marketing, if you're doing it right, when you open your mouth, you should be pointing at a tool." Elite prospectors are good traffic cops. They direct people to sources of information.

The same process works with your "cold" prospects. When you've met someone socially and have come away with their phone number, you let a short amount of time elapse and then you call that person back. You can say, "Hey, Sue, I'm giving you a call – we met last Monday night at the party. You were telling me about your saber-toothed tiger. Do you remember me?" Right away in Sue's mind, she's thinking, "Oh, talking with him was great. He let me talk about myself. I'm so happy to hear from him." From there you can go into the same process as calling your warm market prospects. After you talk about her interests for a few minutes and there's an appropriate pause, you can then say, "Hey, Sue, listen. I've gotten involved in a business recently," or "I've been involved in a business for a while, and your personality is the same as some of the most successful people I work with. I'd love your opinion. Can you do me a favor and take a look at this business for me? It just involves looking at a Web site." Of course she'll say yes.

Contrast this to those times when you have a sense that someone would be great in your business, but when you call them back, you're never able to reach them, or they never call you back. They're thinking, "Oh yeah, there's that network marketing guy. He wants to get me involved in a pyramid." But if you follow my strategy, you'll never have that happen again.

So what happens next? You meet for your scheduled appointment either on the phone or in person a few days later. Always make it a few days later; this gives you time to hook up with somebody else who you can bring with you to the appointment or have available by phone.

The Follow-Up Appointment

After you build some more rapport with your prospect, you ask them, "So, what did you think of the Web site?" Ninety percent of the individuals you prospect in your business will not have looked at the Web site. But that's okay, it doesn't matter; you're expecting this. You say next, "I've arranged for Ken, one of my business partners, to talk to you. Hold on for a second." Call Ken and say, "Hey, Ken, I've got John here. He's a really amazing guy." Openly compliment your prospect – this strokes his or her ego. But you have to mean it. Seriously – if you don't like people, don't join a network marketing business. Be sincere and mean what you say. The bottom line is that you must always take your prospects seriously. Remember things about them. Take notes on them. Truly have a desire to be their friend, and your prospecting will go through the roof.

Introducing your upline enables another person to answer all your prospect's questions, go over the details of the business, and bring them to a logical conclusion. Your job is simply to direct your prospect to the information and then get somebody else to fill in the gaps.

Why do I stress this? I could give you as great an explanation about our product as anybody. I've made a very significant amount of money with it. I can talk about our founders as well as anybody. But I don't do it because the person I'm prospecting can't do it. Later on, I want to be able to say to them, "Listen, Erica. You can do this. Look how easy it is. Look at me, I didn't even mention the business to you." This is true duplication.

The Point of Logical Conclusion

By the end of the conversation, your prospect will have reached a logical conclusion. They can conclude one of three things:

1. "Yes, I like the business; I'm ready to join."
2. "Maybe… I'm not sure. Maybe I'll try the product."
3. "No, I'm not interested."

If they say yes, you literally spin them around – you take them from the narrow end of the funnel and put them right at the top of the funnel again. Now they begin to build their list, introduce the business to their friends, and utilize the same three-step process: the initial call, the invitation to view a Web site, and a follow-up meeting on the phone or in person. And you just keep repeating this process.

Once you've built that list, keep it going. You're going to be attending meetings. You're going to be in society. You're going to get busy in life. The best prospectors in network marketing are out in the world, always meeting new people. Plan to attend some networking events. Go to your company's functions. Get to know people. Just get out there in society. If you increase your exposure to the world, you're going to increase your list.

When I changed my strategy and started using this process, everybody I brought onto my team began to do the same thing. I used the people above me for third-party validation, and the people I brought in used me. Everything started falling into place, and my checks started increasing.

Handling the Nos

What do you do when somebody says no? Call that person once a month, just to say hello. If you contact that person once a month, you will have incredible success in network marketing, even if they continue to say no. And if you've done this the right way, you'll never have to worry about anybody being offended by the process.

Out of all the people that have said no to me, at least 50 percent of them eventually said yes to me. The first time I called my friend Mitzi in Florida three and a half years ago, she said no to me. I called her the next month and didn't even mention my business. I just followed up with her every single month, just to say hello. Of course, I was taking great notes on what was going on in our conversations so I'd remember a couple of little points to bring up. I'd just say, "Hey, Mitzi, I'm checking in. I've really appreciated building a friendship with you, and I want to keep that friendship going. How are you doing? How's it going with your three-eyed toad?"

But when you call, remember that you are just building a friendship. Don't mention the business again. Call once a month until the day you catch them on the right day. Remember that roulette wheel – you don't know when it's going to hit that green zero. You might spin that ball a hundred times around that wheel before it hits the green zero, but it *will* eventually hit the green zero every single time.

Repetition

Focus on just using the same system over and over again. Call your prospects once a month. You'll get so many people into your funnel, into your world, that it's going to be hard to communicate with them all on a monthly basis. You can use e-cards, or you can send them a brief little email. And every two months or so when you're talking to them, you can say, "Hey, listen, my business is still going great. Are you in a different space right now?" Just listen to what they say. What happened with Mitzi is that one month when I called her, her family was moving from Gainesville to Tampa Bay, and she was open to the idea of a new business. The timing was perfect, and she ended up joining my business.

Handling Objections Equals Losing Friends

One of my pet peeves in this industry is "handling objections." It's something I never, ever do. Now, don't get me wrong – if somebody's got a question about the business or they need clarification on something, I'm happy to answer them. But handling objections is a science that's sometimes taught in our industry to mean that if you've got a silver tongue and you can spin it around a ball and tie a double-half-twisted-loop knot in the back, you're going get somebody to join every single time.

In my book, HANDLING OBJECTIONS EQUALS LOSING FRIENDS. A millionaire is somebody who's created a million friends. If you build a million friends, you'll make millions of dollars. Let's say you're leading a prospect through the process, and, after taking a look at the business, they say, "No thanks, I'm not interested." They go on to say that it sounds too much like a pyramid. You tell them, "Well, our government is a true pyramid. The president's at the top, the vice president is below him, and everybody else is below there, and it all works well." While this might be clever (and even true), you're contradicting their mindset.

Or somebody might say to you, "Oh, I don't have the time." The age-old classic answer to this objection is, "Well, you don't need the time. Busy people get things done." What you have to realize is that all of those excuses aren't the real reasons why they aren't joining. The real reason they decided not to join is that it just wasn't the right day. Just keep spinning the wheel!

If you want to be able to call that person month after month after month and continue building a friendship, don't handle objections. Instead, say to the person, "Listen, I really appreciate you looking at this for me. Your friendship is more important to me than making money, so let's just leave it at that." Then continue your conversation.

You might want to prod the person a little bit. You might say, "Would you mind telling me why?" or "Is there anything that I missed in my explanation to you that could assist you?" But if they give you a straight-out objection, you make the decision to either "handle an objection" at the risk of losing friends, or just continue to build the friendship.

Here's an example. Let's say you have a specific opinion on a matter, and I have the opposite opinion. In conversation, I oppose your opinion, and I become adamant about my views. I handle your objection, or I contradict your belief. If somebody has a belief or opinion and you contradict it, how conducive is that to making friends? If I'm prospecting you, and you've got a different opinion and I contradict it, are you going to like me? Absolutely not!

Handling objections might be great for those salespeople who can sell ice to an Eskimo, but the average person isn't like that. If we can teach average people to build friendships, it keeps giving them a chance to roll that ball around the wheel over and over again by just calling their prospects once a month. The key is to stay in touch regularly. This provides more and more chances to contact them on the right day.

Use a little spreadsheet to keep track of your calls so you know when to call your prospects, or create a reminder in your agenda or PDA to keep you on track. You'll be surprised at how much your prospecting results will increase. Honor people and build friendships, and they'll sign up when it's the right day for them every single time. This is really what the term "service to others" means. It's all about trust, respect, and partnership.

The Truth about Duplication

During my first couple of years in network marketing, I managed to master the whole area of recruiting, and I had a lot of success. Yet it has always frustrated me that, in spite of my best attempts to assist people to recruit the right way, the amount of people that become successful prospectors and recruiters has been miniscule.

My mentors always told me that some people just aren't cut out for being successful recruiters. My mentors felt that many people aren't willing to look in the mirror, they're not willing to be coachable, their why isn't big enough – but I couldn't buy into that. What about being able to duplicate – what about having a duplicatable system?

In my own recruiting, I've always done two basic things. The first one is that I go online and search the Internet for leads. I'll go to Google and target a specific city. Then I'll type in "network marketers LA" or "real estate agents LA." This is how I generate leads, and then I'll just call them and ask them if they'd like to take a look at a business.

The second thing I do is that wherever I go locally, I collect business cards from bulletin boards or the fish bowl at a restaurant or a hotel. I call those people and say, "Hey, I got your business card from the restaurant at the hotel," and then ask them if they are open to looking at a business. These two prospecting techniques have worked extremely well for me.

But one day during a training I was conducting for thirty or forty of my reps, I found myself wondering why, although I thought my approach was duplicatable, I wasn't actually duplicating. As I was speaking, I suddenly stopped in mid-sentence. I had just finished saying, "You know, this whole thing is really duplicatable," and then I stopped and said, "You know what? It's not." I had an aha moment: Recruiting and prospecting skills are *not* duplicatable.

Here's the problem. Most trainers in network marketing train based on what *they* do. An Internet recruiter trains people how to recruit on the Internet. The relationship-based recruiter trains people how to build relationships. And they all say that their systems are duplicatable.

Procurement and Processing

I really believe that the biggest reason so many people don't do well in this industry is that they do not understand this key point: Prospecting is not an event; it's a sequence of events. There are two main parts to prospecting: one is *procurement* and the other is *processing*.

Procurement means to gather, to collect, to get things organized, to obtain. Procurement is the lead generation side of prospecting: How do you find the people? The other side of the equation is processing: What do you do with those leads?

Here's the difference. There *is* a duplicatable side to our business. You have to be duplicatable, but only one of the two parts can be duplicated – the processing side. Procurement, the lead generation side, is individualistic in nature. The way I generate leads works well for me, but what if it doesn't fit your personality? What if I just forget about you because I don't think you can do it, but in actuality the only problem is that you've never found a way to generate leads that fits your style? But what if we just allow people to be free and to individualize how they generate leads? Once someone has generated some leads, then they can learn to duplicate the processing side of it.

We've already covered the processing side of prospecting. You put leads through the three-step process (the funnel) and they come out a yes, a no, or a maybe. It's the procurement side that is tied to your personality. Ever since I realized this, I've shared the twelve most popular ways to generate leads. I always start everybody the same way. I get them going in the business, they create a master list, and I do an interval meeting.

You start processing through the people you know – that's duplicatable, but I don't know of anyone who has earned a seven figure annual income in this industry based *only* on the people that they know. This makes the procurement side extremely essential.

I like to share the top twelve ways to generate leads in this business with my new reps. I give them the basics and then ask them which one they'd like to try first. My theory is that everyone can find one or two ways to generate leads that are comfortable for them. (You'll find a list of the twelve ways to generate leads at the end of this chapter.)

Automate the Core Task

Automating the core task is essential if you're going to be a master network marketing prospector and recruiter. Even though I struggled with personality issues, prospecting was second nature to me – it was automatic. One of the essential qualities of great leaders in our industry is that they've learned to automate the core task of prospecting.

The important thing is procurement. If you can find a couple ways to generate leads that you just do naturally, the whole business will become easier for you. Then anytime you're out locally, you've already identified the easiest ways for you to prospect, and you can do it spontaneously.

But what if you can't identify with the way your upline is recruiting? How will you ever become successful? You haven't found your groove. This is because the procurement side is individualistic in nature. Your unique personality has to connect with the right lead generation technique.

When I work with a new person now, I run them through the basics of connecting with their warm market, and then instead of saying, "Hey, try collecting business cards," I say, "Okay, this next part is individualistic in nature. That means it's got to fit your personality, so I'm not going to jam something down your throat. Let's start with these twelve options; let's experiment with them a little bit and see what we can come up with that fits your personality."

I believe that more people would have been successful in this industry over the years if somebody explained to them that only part of the prospecting process is duplicatable. The most important part is *not* duplicatable. You have to find something that fits *your* personality. That's what happened to me. In the very beginning, I found a couple of ways to generate leads that were tied to who I was and felt completely comfortable, and this allowed the whole process to become automatic for me.

Find Your Zone

I've been in this industry for a long time, and I have never heard anyone explain it this way before. As you read this, I hope that you experience a tangible sense of relief. When you realize that you can find ways to generate leads that you're comfortable with, ways that truly work for you, your business starts to become fun!

This is all about getting into your zone with procurement. You can duplicate the three-step process exactly, but until you are comfortable with procurement, you won't be in the zone to process properly. All along, I think we've focused on the wrong roadblock. It's not that people don't want to follow the three-step process; it's simply that they haven't found a way to generate leads that fits their personality.

Once you get into your zone, you'll find it much easier to stay focused on your core task – prospecting!

Twelve Ways to Generate Leads

1. Internet search engines (Google, Yahoo, etc.)
2. Buying leads
3. Collecting business cards
4. Print advertising (newspapers, flyers, local journals)
5. Online advertising
6. Referrals
7. Car ads (advertising, wrapping)
8. Email blasting
9. Social networking (Facebook, Myspace, LinkedIn, etc.)
10. Specialty programs
11. Local social and community groups
12. Extended friends

Have a Why That Makes You Cry

My Best Friend and Biggest Supporter

Family Holiday

The Reason that I Live

Flying in Style to Indonesia

Ken's Dream Cars Outside the House

Dad and Kids

Ken and Julie's Dream Home

Posing with Friends and Dream Cars

Ken, Kevin & Sue Taking a Tour of the Grand Canyon

Shopping in Chicago with Friends

The Dunn Family with Juan Carlos and Hortensia on Mexican Holiday

Building with Friends in Japan

Have a Why That Makes You Cry

Japanese Leaders

Leadership Photo in Jakarta Indonesia

With Indonesian Leaders at Major Company Convention

Ken Teaching about Core Task at Convention

Prospecting Training

Hanging Out with Friends at a Max Training Event

Training

Lovers

Top Award

Addressing the Convention

Ken and Julie Receiving Company's Top Enroller Award

Celebrating the Convention

Have a Why That Makes You Cry

Ken and Julie at Company's Diamond Associate Gala Dinner

Indonesian Reps

US Reps

6

Have a Why That Makes You Cry

"You must remain focused on your journey to greatness."
LES BROWN

I've always been extremely laser-focused on success because I've *never* forgotten what my childhood was like, and the biggest driving factor and motivator in my life today is making sure my kids don't ever experience that. The reason I stay focused is that my why is bigger than anything in my life. Even now, I can't think about my own upbringing and how much I don't want my kids to go through what I experienced without getting emotional.

You might be able make $10,000 a month in income without an insurmountable why, but you'll never get to $100,000 a month unless you have a reason buried deep within you that drives you to make this happen. Do yourself a favor: Have more than one – have several. I have two that drive me every single day.

One of the things that I found amazing about the inspirational leaders that I studied is that they all have huge whys. If you dig into their lives, you will see it for yourself. I would challenge you to use Google to look into Warren Buffett, Steve Jobs, Bill Gates, or John F. Kennedy, and discover for yourself what drives them.

Powerful Examples

I'll give you a really quick example of how powerful a why can be. Let me paint a picture for you. Imagine you are walking downtown on your way to an appointment. You're on your way to a restaurant to meet your college-age son, and you have just enough time to get there.

Now, as you round the corner, you come upon absolute mayhem. All you can see is emergency vehicles and people scattered everywhere. There's been a head-on collision in the middle of the road, and you are shocked because you can see a pair of legs pinned underneath the front tire of one of the cars. You stand there with everyone else, and you say, "What's going on here?" Someone replies, "Oh, gosh, this guy was crossing the road, and these cars, man, *boom!* The fire trucks are coming right now." And everybody says, "Okay, they'll get him out. He's probably dead anyway."

Suddenly you think, *Oh, I'd better go find my son.* You want to see that he's there. You run to the restaurant (he should be there by now) – and you can't find him. You go back to the accident scene and take a second look, and out of the corner of your eye, you recognize your son's shoes! What happens next? You are overcome by instant terror. Imagine it now…. Can you feel the knot in your throat as you read this? Like a flash of light, in the blink of an eye you are over by the car, lifting with all your strength. You manage to lift the car a foot off the ground just as the fire department arrives and the vehicle is removed from the lifeless body. As the car is removed, you realize that it is not your son! Instantly you are overcome with emotion, and you stand back against a nearby wall to collect yourself. Just as you regain your composure, your son appears and gives you a big hug, almost as if he realized what has just happened to you.

If your reason is strong enough, you can do anything you put your mind to. It has been proven again and again throughout the ages that human beings can sustain incredible pain and accomplish unbelievable tasks if the reason why is big enough. I have told this story many times in front of crowds as large as ten thousand to illustrate what someone can do if the reason for doing it is big enough.

One of men I respect the most in the world today is Greg Fullerton, an accomplished businessman and public speaker. He tells a profound story to illustrate what people will do if their reasons are big enough. He paints an incredibly vivid picture of standing on top of one of the World Trade centers in New York. Picture it – feel it. You're standing up there in the midst of gale force winds as the buildings themselves sway back and forth in the breeze beneath your feet. Did you know that the trade center buildings used to sway between four-to-eight feet, depending on the strength of the wind? They were designed to do this.

Now imagine that there is a steel I-beam (the type used in building construction) stretched between the two buildings right over the New York streets. The I-beam is about four inches wide. Can you feel it? The wind is blowing... the buildings are swaying, and the beam is loosely floating as it sits there. Now imagine that you are on one building at the edge of the I-beam, and there is a man standing on the opposite building at the other end of the beam. The man tells you that he will pay you $10,000 to walk across the beam without any support. Would you do it? Obviously not! One wrong step, one gust of wind, and you're gone. But what if the man offered you $100,000 to cross the beam? Would you cross then?

Now, what if the man was standing on the other tower, the wind blowing so hard that it made your hair stand up, and he was holding one of your children over the edge of the tower. As he clung to your child with one hand, he yelled at you, "Cross the beam right now, or I'll drop your child!" Obviously, every parent reading would be halfway across that beam before the man finished his sentence. It is amazing what can be accomplished when the reason is strong enough.

There are countless examples out there about what people have done in the face of adversity, when their why is big enough. What would you be willing to do for your children, your spouse, your parents?

I am sure that some of you read the last couple of stories very skeptically. There is always going to be someone that just won't believe. I was one of those people. During my fifteen years of policing, I was one of the most skeptical people in the world. I was very jaded and dark-humored. At the same time, I was constantly amazed at what people would do if their reason was strong enough.

He Ripped a Car Door Off with His Bare Hands...

I'm writing this chapter during a sixteen-hour flight from Singapore to Los Angeles, and I just recalled another story that demonstrates extreme human ability in the face of adversity.

In May of 2000, I was living in Borden, Ontario for a couple of months while I took a policing course. My family was living over eighteen hours away in Halifax, Nova Scotia. On the May long weekend that year, my partner Mark and I decided that we would drive to Halifax and surprise our families with a weekend visit. It would be a painfully long drive, but we would share the driving time in order to travel nonstop.

Have a Why That Makes You Cry

At about 4:00 pm, we were driving along Canada's busiest highway, Highway 401 just outside of Kingston, Ontario. Rock music on the radio played loudly as we headed for home. Mark was driving, and I was drifting off to sleep in the passenger seat. Just as I was zoning out, Mark hit the brakes hard and yelled, "Holy cow!" I looked up just in time to see an eighteen-wheeler jack-knife into the oncoming traffic, hit six cars, and then head into the ditch that divided the east and westbound lanes.

The ditch was about six feet lower than the surface of the road. Even though the big rig was now on its side, it hit the ditch doing at least forty miles an hour. Because of the lower grade, when the truck came out of the ditch into our lane, it was launched into the air. I remember this event like it was happening again right before my eyes. What happened in seconds comes back to me in minutes. I watched the truck as if in slow motion. Four p.m. on the Friday of a long weekend means that the highway was jam-packed. That rig (that was hauling steel) came back to the road, landed on another seven cars before sliding to a stop in an adjacent field. The resulting scene was apocalyptic. Immediately our training kicked in, and Mark and I jumped out of the car and ran to the scene.

Along with several other Good Samaritans, we spent the next three hours tending to the injured. It was horrific. To this date, it is still the worst accident ever to occur on the 401. Many people lost their lives that day. After everything calmed down, a police officer took a statement from me for his records. As I recounted what had occurred and my observations, he walked me through the scene so I could point things out to him as we spoke. I recounted how I approached one of the cars that the rig had landed on and found a woman unconscious with massive injuries in the passenger seat. I attempted to locate a pulse and realized that there was none. Due to the recent timing of the accident, Mark and I made a decision to remove the woman from the car and begin CPR. As I was explaining how we set the woman on the ground, the officer interrupted me and asked me where we got the "jaws of life" (a mechanical air compression based tool used to rip cars apart in accident situations). I told him we didn't have this tool. In reply, he asked, "Well, how did you remove the car door?"

I looked at the door, shocked. Another of the Samaritans who was standing beside us interjected, "You guys ripped the door off – don't you remember?" My jaw dropped. I had no recollection of ripping the door off that car. As the observer explained, Mark walked up to the car and confirmed that we had ripped the door of the car off. He explained that because the door had been badly damaged, we couldn't get it open, and so we tore it off. I was so intensely focused on starting CPR on the victim that I didn't realize that we had ripped the door off. Our adrenaline was running so fast through our bodies in the middle of this crisis situation that we were able to complete a superhuman, normally impossible task.

Focus on Your Passion

Warren Buffett is an extraordinary example of someone who knows his why and has accomplished great success because of it. He knew what he wanted and how to get there from a young age. Even as a child, Buffett's prized possession was a coin-changer, and when his father offered to take him on a trip, young Warren chose the New York Stock Exchange as his destination. Not long after this, he read a book called *One Thousand Ways to Make $1000*, and he told his friends he planned to be a millionaire by the time he was thirty-five. This, remember, was back in the tough economy of 1941, but Buffett was sure he could achieve this.

Buffett himself has said that he attributes his success to focus. In a book called *Snowball: Warren Buffett and the Business of Life* by Alice Schroeder (the title comes from Buffett's advice on success:

Find some wet snow and a really long hill), the author says, "He ruled out paying attention to almost anything but business – art, literature, science, travel, architecture – so that he could focus on his passion." Warren Buffett has a powerful why and a powerful focus – so much so that when you hear his name, you immediately think "investing."

My Own Why

As a kid in grade school, there were opportunities to go on class field trips to some pretty cool places – Spain, for instance, and other trips overseas to Europe. My family could never afford to send me, so I never was able to go on these trips. Instead, I'd be put into a lower grade for the week, where I'd be tormented, made fun of, and criticized by the other kids.

Our family was so poor that my folks couldn't afford to buy clothes for all of us, so we took advantage of Salvation Army. I remember being so embarrassed when the other kids ridiculed and made fun of me for wearing shabby clothes to school when I was ten, eleven, twelve... by the time I was thirteen I used to actually steal clothes. I'm not proud of this, and the only reason I'm mentioning it is to give you an idea of what really drives me today.

By the time I was sixteen, I had decided that if I wanted anything, I had to go out and get it myself. At one point, my shoes literally were so worn that they had holes in the bottom. I decided to go to the department store to "exchange" them. At the time everyone was wearing Converse basketball shoes, those red-and-white high tops. This was back in the days of Doctor Jay, and everybody was wearing them.

I tried on a pair, and then I walked out with them on, leaving my old shoes behind. As I was leaving, a guy came up and grabbed me by the arm, saying, "I'm with the department store security. I need you to come with me." I just thought it was all over. My dad was going to find out, and life as I knew it was going to end. I was scared to death.

The security officer said, "I know you stole those watches. What did you do with them?" He had no idea that I was wearing the sneakers – he actually thought I had stolen something else. I adamantly denied stealing the watches, sweating bullets the whole time. Then my father showed up. Now, my dad was a very stern military man. The security officer began to tell him what happened. Finally, they realized that I had nothing to do with stealing the watches, and we walked away.

That one moment saved my life. For many children at a young age, when they get away with things like this, it's the beginning of a career in crime. But in my case, on that day I decided that I needed more, I wanted more, and I was going do something about it.

To this day, I remember those feelings from over twenty-five years ago, and wanting something different for myself and my family still propels me forward – definitely a why that makes me cry!

My Dad Gives Me Strength

I am the son of a naval officer. My dad served in the Canadian navy his entire adult life, over thirty-seven years. In 2006, my dad lost his life to a vicious disease called ALS (Lou Gehrig's disease). This is the most pathetic, indiscriminating disease known to man. Prior to contracting ALS, my dad was one of the healthiest people that I knew. In 2005, Dad got a cold that never went away. After a couple of months, he went to the hospital for a checkup and was diagnosed with ALS. His health deteriorated quickly.

I was sitting in the room with my mom and dad when his doctor delivered the news. He said, "He has only a few months to live." Just writing these words has caused me to tremble. Just over a year later, I sat beside my dad's hospital bed. The disease had robbed him of his body. He was 140 pounds lighter, and he had lost the ability to speak, to use his hand and legs, or to communicate in any way. The pain was out of control. My dad passed away that night at fifty-four years old. It's not fair; he didn't deserve it. In my fifteen years of police work, I knew many people who deserved something like this, but my dad didn't. So far, no one knows what causes ALS.

A few months after my dad died, I was approached by a friend to look at a new network marketing company. It was a company being started by Steven K. Scott, Greg Fullerton, and Fred Ninow. They had discovered a nutritional product – a capsule that radically increases the production of glutathione in the body. Glutathione is the body's master antioxidant, and it is the only antioxidant produced in the cells. I knew what glutathione was, and I was excited by the idea. I jumped at the opportunity right away. My excitement was huge, because I knew in the back of my mind that if my dad's glutathione levels had been higher, his cells might have been strong enough to fight the disease – or maybe he might have never contracted it.

I was really excited about this new opportunity because it would give me a reason to educate people about glutathione and teach them how important it was to build up the body's natural ability to produce it. I can't bring my dad, back but I can definitely help to prevent others from potentially getting serious diseases. An ounce of prevention is worth a pound of cure.

I would not want anyone to experience the pain that I went through watching my dad die.

You Will Make Sacrifices Along the Way...

By the time my flight lands in Los Angeles, I will have traveled over 180,000 miles on airplanes this year. I will have spent over 100 nights in hotels. I am saddened to disclose this, but I just missed my son Matthew's first piano recital last weekend while I was in Jakarta. I have missed birthdays, anniversaries, and many other special occasions while I have been traveling and building my business.

This is very painful for me. I can't watch movies on the plane that have kids in them without crying because of how much I miss Laura, Matthew, and Julie when I'm away. You need to know that any greatness you achieve will involve sacrifices. Your why has to be strong enough to endure the pain.

Believe me, it is easier to give up, but what would that cause?

Personally, I cannot give up. My whys are too important! I NEVER want my children to live the life that I lived growing up, and I don't want their children to live that life either. And don't get me wrong! When I get home tonight, it is going to be complete family time. We'll make up for the time that I am away. And because of the power of residual income and network marketing, I will only work hard for a couple more years and then most likely retire at forty. How does that sound?

Discover Your Own Why

Your ability to succeed in achieving your desired success is directly related to your awareness of *why* you want that success. These underlying reasons, beliefs, and values form your core motivation. They are the driving force to ultimately release your potential and personality. Basically, your attitudes and your zeal to succeed are the external expression of what's going on internally with you – strong emotions that may evolve out of hurt, needs, or aspirations.

It's important to write out your why. Dig deep within yourself to discover your own reasons for pursuing success. Why did you get into network marketing in the first place? What made you want to start your own business? Is it because you wanted to be your own boss? Did you want more freedom? More time to spend with your family? More money? Whatever your why is, this is what will keep you going when things aren't going well.

Once you have your why in writing, read it – out loud – every day. Read it when you wake up in the morning and again in the evening before going to sleep. Doing this on a daily basis will assist you to cement your why deep down in your heart and mind. You might even choose to rewrite your why every morning. This can really keep you focused, and keep your mind open for new opportunities throughout the day. It is unbelievable what this activity can do for your daily motivation, because it will move you to action.

Don't keep your why to yourself, either. Sharing your why with others sends your convictions into overdrive! This will drive you into massive action, and you will supercharge others too.

Hints on Finding Your Real Why

1. Your why should make your cry.
2. Look back through your life, reflecting on everything.
3. Be ready – your why may come to you when you least expecting it!
4. Determine the one thing that causes you the most stress today, that brings tears   to your eyes – the one thing that will be gone once you succeed in network marketing.
5. Your why is the reason you keep going even when you want to quit.

7

Improve Your Communication

*"Effective communication is 20 percent what you know and 80
percent how you feel about what you know."*
Jim Rohn

If you've ever seen Steve Jobs, the charismatic cofounder
of Apple Computer, give a keynote address, you'll undoubtedly
agree that he's one of the most extraordinary speakers in corporate
America. Jobs learned a long time ago that a leader must be part
evangelist and part brand spokesperson.

Steve Jobs is magnificent to watch. What makes his presentations
so dazzling? Steve Jobs does not sell bits of metal; he sells an
experience. Instead of focusing on mind-numbing statistics, he
sells benefits. When introducing a new Apple product, he clearly
explains what it means to the consumer. He reviews and rehearses
his material. That sense of casual informality that he portrays only
comes after grueling hours of practice.

Jobs has an infectious enthusiasm. He exudes passion and energy.
There is no better example of this passion than the famous story of
how he convinced John Sculley to lead Apple in the mid '80s by
asking him, "Do you want to sell sugared water all your life or do
you want to change the world?" The former Pepsi executive chose
the latter, and although their partnership ultimately failed, it reflects
Jobs' sense of mission – a mission that he communicated consistently
in the early years of Apple and still communicates today.

In my own life, I had no choice but to become a communicator. Ever since I was eighteen years old, I've had to collect facts. I had to learn to assemble those facts in a way that made sense, and then I learned to present them in a way that people could understand. Over the course of fifteen years, I must have testified in court thousands of times, and I learned to get my point across in a way that communicated all the details in a succinct way. I discovered how to be very accurate in a short amount of time.

Think for a second about someone you know that is extremely successful. I'll bet they are great speakers. Their ability to speak is most likely captivating. When I studied that amazing group of seven leaders, I was not surprised to learn that all seven were great speakers. It is essential to be a great communicator if you want to be successful; it's vital that you are understood. I truly believe that anyone can become a great speaker if he or she really works at it. If you want to be extremely successful in network marketing, it will be easier if you can communicate well. Don't get me wrong – you can become successful even if you are not a good talker, but it will just take longer and be a bit more painful.

Be Detailed, But Don't Overcommunicate

Many people overexplain things, and I was no exception. In court, I always knew when I'd gone too far when I'd see the judge's eyes glaze over, and I'd realize that he was tuned out to what I was trying to say. I wanted so desperately for the judge to really understand what I was saying that often I'd repeat myself six or seven times in the process, which was *not* effective.

To effectively communicate with someone, communicate the details, but stop after you've said something the first time. I can't tell you the number of people that I've met who start talking and just keep talking for the sake of being heard.

This is called *overcommunicating.*

Instead, be cognizant of the fact that you only have to tell your story once. You only have to communicate the details once. If you communicate them concisely and clearly, you'll be understood the first time. *How* you say things is just as important as *what* you say. If you become skilled at how you say things, you won't have to repeat yourself over and over again. I encourage you to practice this. If you are someone who oversells a point, then begin to do things differently. For instance, intentionally stop after you've said something the first time. It will be uncomfortable for you in the beginning, but you'll get good at it eventually, and it will become second nature.

Do you know someone who talks so much that it becomes painful? Even the mere thought of this person causes you pain. I know several people that just talk way too much. I'd like to just reach out and tell them, but unfortunately those people would be offended to hear me say this, so hopefully they'll read this book. In the past, I have actually told some people that they talk too much, but it never comes across right. This is a sensitive topic, but people who talk too much are hurting themselves.

When you have spoken clearly and concisely, how do you know if someone has really understood what you've said? Ask a question. This way, you'll know if a certain point requires more clarification.

Use Stories to Communicate

One thing I observed in all of my mentors is that they talk in stories. Whenever they would try and get a point across with me, they would share related experiences and tell a story around the point. Instead of just telling me to go in a certain direction or do something, they would share a story about a related experience, a story about themselves or someone they knew. *"You know, I have a friend that went through that exact situation (explain the story next and then share how your friend inevitably did).* You might think that it's awkward to speak that way, or that it would be easier to just get to the point. That's what I thought too, and the way I communicated in my first year in network marketing was always curt and to the point. And you already know what that got me: a membership to the NFL (No Friends Left)!

How I Became an Effective Communicator

I barely got out of high school. I'm pretty sure that I only graduated because one of my teachers felt pity for me. I never went to university. Literature was never my strong suit, but because I spent fifteen years in policing, every day I collected details, and I had to communicate those details to a judge or a jury so that they could understand them.

It was essential that I developed the skill of effectively communicating so a judge felt that I truly knew what I was talking about and believed me. Taking the oath before testifying was no guarantee that a particular judge would find me credible. After thousands of hours giving evidence, watching juries and judges, I realized that they responded as much to the tone I used and the way I said things as to the actual words I said. They listened very closely to my words, but there was much more to it than that. I'm sure the judges made decisions in court based on the presence of fact, but I'm also positive that the way I said things didn't hurt me.

I didn't become a master communicator by taking a course or reading a book; it was just thousands of hours of experience spent communicating. I learned firsthand that much of what passes for communication is really a very cheap imitation. Then, when I studied those seven leaders – as well as Steve, Fred, and Greg – I realized that they were (and are) really great communicators. I realized that if I was going to become the successful inspirational leader that I wanted to be, I had to become a great communicator.

I knew that I already had it going for me. I wish you could *hear* me say these words because you'd feel the tone and intonation in every aspect of them that is so important. In order to be a great communicator, you have to know what you're talking about. This comes from reading and studying and communicating, over and over again. In our industry, communication involves attending events and becoming an active listener. Repeated listening makes you a better communicator, because the information you're communicating becomes more comfortable the more you hear it.

In court, we were always taught to be very concise. I remember my police sergeant saying, "Speak less; say more." When I got involved in network marketing, I saw how well this advice fit. If one of the secrets to success is getting people to know you, like you, and trust you, communication is absolutely key to this process. It's being conscious of your tone of voice; it's the way you talk and what you say, being careful not to overcommunicate.

Master the Art of Communication

Always be aware of the person you're talking to. When you're attempting to build a relationship with somebody during the recruiting process, ask open-ended questions. People love this, because we all love to talk about ourselves. Don't make the fatal flaw of interrupting them. During the process, if you ask somebody a question and then halfway through the answer you interrupt the person to talk more about yourself, you'll never get that person to like you. Instead, you'll offend that person, and he or she will never join your business. Not interrupting people is paramount to becoming a successful communicator.

If you are someone with a foreign accent, make sure you are clearly understood. Many people have such strong accents that they're hard to understand. If you want to be successful in any business endeavor, you have to be understood. If your accent is so strong that it's hard for people to understand you, there are specific coaches that can assist you to develop a clearer use of your language and clean up your accent when you're speaking to other people.

Actors are an example of those who work at eliminating any trace of a foreign accent, depending on the role they are playing. Actors work with voice coaches and communications coaches all the time. Why not network marketers? You can find a local voice coach or a speaking coach online, and you'll discover that many of them are very reasonably priced.

Sidney Poitier is one actor who was determined to become a success, and working on his accent was a key part of his strategy. His is a rags-to-riches story: He was raised in the Bahamas, the son of a tomato farmer. When he was sixteen years old, he set out for New York City, where he took a series of jobs, including dishwasher, longshoreman, butcher's assistant, porter, construction worker, salad washer, drugstore clerk, and soldier. In 1945 he decided to take a stab at acting. He joined the American Negro Theatre, where he learned to eliminate his West Indian accent. Intent on transforming himself, Poitier practiced constantly, mimicking the voices he heard on the radio. And if you've ever seen Sidney Poitier, I'm sure you'll agree that his deep, rich voice is one of the most memorable things about him.

Singers with foreign accents often lose any trace of an accent while singing. A good example of this is the group Abba. During the first few years of their remarkable career, none of them spoke enough English to place an order at McDonald's, but when you hear them sing, they are much easier to understand than many native English speakers. It's crucial for actors and singers to develop their voices this way because their livelihood depends on it. What makes them great is their ability to do this. Why shouldn't network marketers be just as conscious of this? Our livelihood also depends on our ability to communicate with excellence.

Our business is about prospecting. It's about approaching new people, and often we have to do that on the telephone. Frequently you'll leave a voicemail message. If you talk fast or slur your speech or use some dialect that's hard to understand on the phone, you'll limit your ability to get a call back. In order to get somebody to call you back, speak slowly and clearly. Speak concisely, leaving a short message that's to the point and easy to understand. That will affect the amount of people that call you back.

Become a Professional Storyteller

In our business, we're professional storytellers. We contact people every day, and we're continually building relationships. One of the oldest sayings in this industry is, "Facts tell, stories sell." If you're trying to win somebody's heart, it's based on your ability to tell a story. If you take a look at all the millionaires in network marketing, you'll find that they're all professional storytellers. They tell the story of their company's products, of their opportunities, and of the experiences they've been through in the business.

More crucial than the details of any story is the way it's communicated. The words you use are important, but *how* you use them is even more important. When I tell a story, it's the tone of my voice that creates the excitement people feel when they're listening to me. It's the passion they feel when I talk about my products and my services that gets their attention. This is extremely important. You can talk to any leader in the industry; they'll all tell you the same thing. The top income earners are the best storytellers.

There are two parts to becoming a great storyteller. The first part is the information you're seeking to share. Anybody can get information today just by going on the Internet. The second part is the way you communicate: the way you tell that story, the tones you use, the respect you pay to whoever is listening to you. Be aware of the time. Be aware of your accent and tone. Be aware of how fast or slow you're talking. If you want somebody to really understand what you're saying, repeat one sentence, or a part of a sentence, with the right intonation. How you communicate your story is actually more important than the specific points you make.

Some Tips for Communicating with Prospects

Using Teaser Lines

Teaser lines are small, individual lines about our industry that are used to solicit interest from people in casual conversations. There are all kinds of casual interactions with people where you can end up inviting somebody to look at your business. But when you first meet somebody in a casual setting, don't invite that person to look at your business right away. Get to know them first. As part of my own inviting and prospecting process, I often start conversations with people and just get to know them a bit. Whenever and wherever you can, simply open up and talk to people.

Power Lines

Power lines are one-liners that you use to instantly create interest in evaluating your opportunity, and at the same time, invite somebody to take a look at your business. As you create your own power lines, make sure they include the following elements:

1. Introduce yourself and what you're doing.
2. Mention the industry and the trend you're involved in.
3. Validate the trend with a little bit of statistical information or media exposure.
4. Highlight a benefit or two that they can achieve if they were to do the same thing as you.
5. Ask a question and make sure you get a yes answer to it. By doing that, you can remove all of the fears or objections they might have.

Communicate Your Way to Success

Developing your communication skills will increase your bank account, so do whatever is required for you to become an effective communicator. Learn to tell great stories. As your network marketing organization grows, you'll be required to speak effectively in public. You'll have lots of opportunities to address groups of people. You'll conduct trainings and coach new business partners. From prospecting to training, communication skills are essential. Good communication skills will increase your confidence as well as your income!

Tips to Improve Your Communication

1. Be detail-oriented in every aspect of your speech; don't overcommunicate.
2. Speak less and say more.
3. Never interrupt anyone else when they are speaking.
4. If you have a strong accent, speak slower.
5. Be sure you know something about the subject you're speaking about.
6. It's okay not to know something or understand a certain point – a strong communicator admits a lack of knowledge right up front.

8

Build Confidence

*"Happiness and self-confidence come naturally when you feel
you are moving and progressing toward becoming the very best
person you can possibly be."*
BRIAN TRACY

Confidence is a quality that is often misunderstood in our business. A few years ago, I was having dinner with a teammate of mine from Florida. During the course of our conversation, he told me that he wasn't happy with his level of success and that he didn't have any credibility. That really struck me because this guy was a really successful entrepreneur; he had tons of credibility in my opinion. He just hadn't been successful in network marketing yet. I realized that what he really meant was that he lacked confidence. He wasn't confident in what he was doing. Often in our industry, people confuse credibility and confidence, and this can be a dream killer.

As my teammate shared his perceived lack of credibility, suddenly a story from my childhood popped into my head, and I shared it with him. When I was in the second grade, I was just a young whippersnapper, and one day I was being bullied by a fellow my age. This young fellow thought he was a tough guy, and we started pushing each other around, and he spat in my face. I was so enraged by this that it just drove me right off the deep end.

I grabbed him, but he managed to get away from me. He knew how angry I was, and he was afraid. He started running, and I ran after him as hard as I could. We ran for several minutes through the school, through the backyard... I just wanted to rip him apart when I grabbed him. He ran around a corner, and as I came around the corner, there he stood – suddenly completely confident with six of his best friends flanking him, three on each side, all staring at me. I stopped in my tracks, and I became instantly afraid. I didn't know what to do.

All seven of these guys now came at me, and I ran without stopping for three miles, all the way back to my house. This experience came into my head as I sat there looking at this incredibly successful entrepreneur who was saying he had no credibility, no confidence. I told him that story. I said, "Listen, as I ran around that corner and saw those guys standing there, I didn't only see that one fellow who had just spat in my face. I saw these seven guys, and I was instantly fearful where I'd been angry before."

I likened that experience to how he should deal with his perceived lack of credibility. You see, the weakest of the bunch was that little guy who had just spat in my face, but now, flanked by his friends, I couldn't even see the little guy – I saw the total of seven boys.

In order to get over your own lack of credibility, use this simple idea based on that story. Make a list of all the great things you have done in your life, and then add to it all the greatest attributes of your personality. Write this list in a single column on the left side of a clean piece of paper. Now, in a second column to the right of that, write down "lack of success in network marketing." What you have to realize is that when people are evaluating you and your network marketing company, they don't see your lack of success. They see all the other stuff. The lack of success is just a point that is stuck in *your* head.

Once I shared this story with my teammate, he got it right away. He created a list of all of his good personality traits and accomplishments in life, and at the top of the list he wrote, *"I have credibility in life."* To this day, he carries that list around with him everywhere, and he reads it several times per day. In fact, he reads it so much that he has forgotten all about the fact that he has not been as successful as he would like to be. Of course, his prospecting and closing has gone up 100 percent.

People are not going to see the little guy in the middle; they will see the group of seven standing before them. Create your own list, and your confidence will go through the roof.

I told my teammate, "Here's the bottom line. You already have everything you require to be successful in this business." I shared with this entrepreneur several things about his own life that were successful. I pointed out several positive qualities about this incredibly successful entrepreneur. He was a millionaire. He was charismatic. He was an incredible entrepreneur. As I was explaining to him how much I respected and appreciated him, I saw his back straighten up, and I saw a huge smile appear on his face.

I asked him, "How do you feel right now, at this moment?"

He said, "I feel great. I know these things are true."

I said, "That's *all* other people see."

Act in Spite of Fear

Even though I've made this sound very simple (and it *is* that simple), there will be times when the telephone sitting in front of you suddenly seems to weigh 100 pounds. I'll let you in on a little secret – even though I had been confident in my other endeavors, I was not at all confident when I began my network marketing career. I was very nervous about calling the first people I called in this business… *but I called them anyway.*

Act in spite of your fear. We all go through this. You have to be able to pick up the phone if you want to get the results. Tell yourself that you're just looking for people that are looking. You have to go through a lot of people. Write this down in big, bold letters: **Eight out of ten people will say no.** If you understand this, then you'll realize that you just need to get through those eight out of ten people, over and over again.

The key to this business is not how much you actually *know*, but how *excited* you are. Success in network marketing is 99 percent attitude and 1 percent aptitude. It doesn't matter if you know anything about your opportunity. All you need to know is that it's the most incredible opportunity in the world. We'd all rather have ignorance on fire than knowledge on ice. Let your excitement fuel your actions, and you'll discover that because you are so excited, you will act with confidence.

Be Passionate!

Be passionate! Passion is fueled by belief. Stay connected to the successful people in your upline so they can assist you to fuel your belief. If you do this, your passion will go up, your belief level will go up, and this will be transmitted through the words you say.

If you're not somebody that is normally pumped up, do whatever you have to do to get yourself pumped up. And then jump into it: "Sue, I'm really excited! I've found a great opportunity that I think will assist me to get where I want to go financially in life, and I want you to hear about it because I think there's something here for you also. When can we get together?" (This is for somebody in your warm market.) Ask them directly – all you want to do is put them in front of the information.

It's Not About the Money

When I think about the seven inspirational leaders that have so impacted my journey, I realize that every one of them was supremely confident in what they were doing, even though every one of them had flaws of one kind or another. You never saw those flaws, though; you looked at them, and you just saw incredible confidence.

Many of you have been in network marketing for many years and have never made a dime. You might be looking at yourself and saying, "I have no credibility because I haven't made money." But here's the thing: credibility doesn't come from the money. I know many people that have gotten into this business that have never made a cent, but they have this natural inherent ability to recruit other people, to connect with other people. Their confident qualities, their successes in life, all their best qualities are shining through. Every time I introduce somebody to my business or I get a chance to coach with somebody, I have them point out all their best qualities. This enables them to recruit with those qualities, with those thoughts in their mind, and they stop worrying about the credibility they perceive isn't there because they haven't made any money yet. They're just limiting themselves with that mindset.

Don't Let Your Limitations Limit You

Let's face it – everybody has limitations. When I get a chance to coach someone, I explore with that person the incredible confidence those seven inspirational leaders have. Even though each of them had limitations in their lives, they didn't let those limitations shine through.

Pierre Trudeau is an example of someone who had unwavering confidence and charisma in the face of strong opponents. Many Canadians, myself included, highly regard him, but he inspired fierce antipathy among those who disagreed with his political decisions and policies. One historian, Michael Bliss, put it this way: "Trudeau is one of the most admired and most disliked of all Canadian prime ministers." Trudeau's confidence had everything to do with him becoming one of the most transformative figures in Canada's history.

Gandhi is another person who recognized the value of confidence. He said, "The history of the world is full of men who rose to leadership, by sheer force of self-confidence, bravery, and tenacity." How's that for some inspired coaching? He's saying you can become a leader, not by being particularly gifted or by the absence of any limitations, but by the sheer force of your own confidence.

Steve Jobs and John F. Kennedy both had severe health issues, but neither of them allowed these limitations to lessen their confidence or their impact. Kennedy had chronic pain and digestive problems his entire adult life. Steve Jobs had a rare form of pancreatic cancer back in 2003 and recently was in the news again when people began questioning his health. They wondered if his cancer had returned or if he'd had a heart attack. Through it all, he confidently continued to do what he does best – lead Apple.

Just like these leaders, the reason why some individuals become so incredibly successful in network marketing and others don't is that, while we all have limitations, while we all lack some type of credibility, those who make it to the top don't let those limitations hold them back. They focus on the things they're really great at and build upon those characteristics.

A vital key to being successful in network marketing is knowing what your strengths are, really focusing on those strengths, and letting those good qualities come through when you're dealing with people. For instance, when you focus on improving your communication skills, defining your why, being detail-oriented, and increasing your gravitational pull, you'll build up other areas of your credibility, even if you're not making money yet.

No matter what our vocation is, we're all learning to master it each and every day. The difference between those of us who create phenomenal results and those who don't is that those of us who do have learned to master creating results based on the skills and strengths we already bring to the table *while* we're developing those other areas that require a bit more attention. And that's exactly what you can do too!

Keys for Building Confidence

- Know your existing strengths and skills.
- Develop and improve any areas that require improvement, always letting your existing qualities shine through.
- Make a list of your greatest personality strengths and your greatest successes in life and carry it around with you.
- Focus on your strengths, not your limitations.

9

Pay Attention to the Details

"A man's accomplishments in life are the cumulative effect of his attention to detail."
JOHN FOSTER DULLES

In this chapter, I'll cover how to develop the ability to be organized and focus on the details of creating a successful network marketing business. Maybe you've just joined a network marketing company, or perhaps you've been in the industry for a while and you're looking for a refresher. Either way, the key to success in this business is getting started properly, and this chapter will spell things out for you.

All of the inspirational leaders I studied were meticulous about how they lived their lives and their callings. For instance, Mother Teresa had a sharp analytical mind and a keen eye for detail. Extremely conscientious, she was efficient and thorough in her work and took pride in a job well done. She was adept at using her hands to create or fix things, and meticulous attention to detail and careful craftsmanship were her forte. Mother Teresa liked to organize, categorize, and arrange everything into a logical system – she was very uncomfortable with disorganization. Besides being a stickler for details, she had a strong desire to continually improve, refine, and perfect. Mother Teresa was especially particular about her diet, hygiene, and health habits; her tastes were simple and understated, yet refined. You'll want to develop a similar attention to details as you set up your business in ways that will allow it to soar.

The Essentials

This is a simple business, and there are only a few essentials required to truly be successful in network marketing. Being organized is right at the top, and equally important is having an efficient system and using it.

In our industry, connecting with people is key, and there are a multitude of details that you'll want to pay attention to if you desire to reach the top. The more detail-oriented you are about the essentials, the less you'll miss opportunities and the faster you'll drive your business forward. I will provide you with strategies for creating a master list of people to contact, and I'll show you how you can continually add to it, many times for free by utilizing the power of the Internet. But in order to really master this business, you must learn to focus on key details and organize your time each day.

When I began my network marketing business, I had no idea how to actually get started properly. I had passion, and yes, ignorance on fire is better than knowledge on ice any day. But if you know the basics, then you can go crazy and build an incredible business – it all starts with the fundamentals. It's a great feeling to introduce people to your company and your products; you get a charge every time you do it. Every time you personally bring somebody new into this industry, you get something out of what that person saw in the industry and what they saw in you.

Building a business in the network marketing industry actually has very little to do with your product, your compensation plan, the timing of a trend, or whether your company is private or public, party plan or direct selling, or internal consumption. People join this business for three reasons: *they know you, they trust you, and they like you.* I first heard this several months after I joined the business, and I wish that I would have heard it at the very beginning of my network marketing career. Understanding these three reasons is the *most important part* of building a strong foundation.

Let's Get Organized

The key to your success is being organized from the day you get started. You're starting a home business! That's it, plain and simple. You must have some space set up for yourself that you can operate from. Understand from day one that you are starting an international enterprise, and in order to do that successfully, you have to set it up properly. If nobody has ever taught you this, you're learning it now. *Get organized.* Once you've designated the space in your house, set up a home office. If you've already got one, set it up properly. The tools of your trade are very simple: a phone, paper and a pen, and the Internet (if you're with an Internet-driven company). Make sure you have these things available and ready for your daily work.

The Home Office

It's vitally important that you designate space in your house that you can call your home office. It doesn't have to be a separate room; it can literally be a space in your kitchen. My first home office was a space in my bedroom. I kept my notes, my pen, my paper, and some price lists for my products on my dresser. I called this my office because that's all I had available at the time for my business, but I took it very seriously, and I treated it with respect. Nothing else got in the way – it was a priority. Eventually I graduated from that space on my dresser to a closet. To this day, my set up is pretty much the same. I have a desk with a computer, a little calculator, some price lists and brochures from my company, a list of my contacts and prospects, my follow-up charts, and my agenda. It's all right there.

If you set yourself up from the start to be ready for success, your chances of achieving that success will be far greater. Then, once you've set up your home office, *get out of the house.* The beautiful thing about this business is that you can do it any way you want. When you start to venture outside of your home to build your business, it's crucial that you are already set up properly for success.

You Are a Master Franchiser

The list of names that you write when you first get started is the foundation of your business. At the same time you write your list, you also have to understand this industry. Regardless of what company you're in, ask yourself, "What is my goal in this company, in this business?" Here's my answer: **You're building an international distribution process**. You're creating a way of moving products from point A to point B, from the manufacturer right to the end consumer. Your goal is to create a network of thousands of people that buy your company's products and either resell them or consume them themselves. This is the key to financial freedom.

Picture yourself as a *master franchiser* – as someone who is opening a new franchise in your state, in your city. Your goal is to get people to buy franchises. The way you make money as a master franchiser is to go out and present your opportunity and your products to people. Your goal at the end of the day is to find people who are willing to invest and open franchises of their own. In this case, it's a micro-franchise, but nonetheless, it's definitely a franchise-like system.

Keep Your Why Close

Be clear from the beginning about *why* you are doing a business like this. I carry a little card around in my wallet every single day, and on that card is a saying. It's a statement I've made to myself about why I'm actually doing this business. To this day, it's amazing the energy that I get sometimes by just looking at this simple card. We're in the most incredible business in the world! Tell yourself that right now, make sure you've written down your why, and keep it with you always.

Is Your Mind in the Game?

Before you contact anybody, get your mind in the game. Your goal has to be very clear to you. You have to picture yourself as already successful. Visualization is a powerful key to success. I'm already where I want to be in my mind, and I get up every single day picturing myself already as a multimillionaire. I picture myself already having assisted thousands of people all around the world to create success for themselves. You have to create the mindset that you're already successful. If you can get yourself into that mindset – and of course you can, it's your choice – then all you have to do each day is go out and show your opportunity to people.

Create Your List

Your list of names is the foundation of your business. Grab a full size piece of paper, sit down, and start writing down the name of every single person you know. I know, it sounds corny. Everyone thinks this at first, but the reason for it is simple. You're looking for people that you think would be great at this business, but the way the human mind works is a little mysterious.

If you were to write a list of only the people you think would be great at this business, you might come up with five or six people. But believe me, you will definitely miss the superstar that will hit the home run that will take you to the next performance bonus level, because this is the way the mind works. You'll literally come up with three or four names immediately, but you'll forget the ones that are the most important, because they might not be the people that you saw in the last twenty-four hours. Your mind will process the people, the thoughts, the ideas that you've had in the last thirty days.

If you're over twenty years old, you've already met over 2,000 people. Your list should contain at least 100-200 people. Here's how you do it: Start by thinking about the people that you know and interact with every day. Don't worry about age; don't worry about gender. Don't worry about whether they would be good at your business. You're just writing names down on paper. That's all there is to it. You'll know when you're done because you won't be able to think of any more people.

Once you get through that first group of names, open up your phone book and go through the alphabet. When you see Smith, think of all the Smiths you know. You'll see Browns and you'll think of a couple more. Think of your doctor, your dentist, and your lawyer. Go through your old high school yearbooks. Trust me, if you do this, you'll have a list you'll never be able to keep up with. I guarantee you'll have over 100 people. Don't worry about phone numbers yet. Now go back through your list and pick out the top twenty people. This is your dream team. Believe me, there will be names among that twenty that would not have appeared on your original list had you just tried to pick out your superstars originally.

Here's the next step: Make that list something that never stops. As you go through your daily life, you'll be driving to your favorite restaurant, and as you go by, you'll see an old friend walk out the door – someone you forgot to put on your list. Every time you come across a new person, add them to your list. Now, as you go through your list and talk to people, don't strike them off the list. Create a supplementary list in addition to this master list. Once you've talked to somebody and they've decided they do or do not want to see your opportunity, refile them and reschedule them accordingly, because if they say no to the business or no to you, that just means no *today*.

A friend of mine that I called the first week I joined my company adamantly said it wasn't the right time for him, and I said very politely, "Do you mind if I keep you informed?" I did that every six months for the next two years, and that same friend joined my company less than a week ago. Never, ever throw somebody away. A no just means no today. It's very important that you understand this.

A Step-by-Step System

A network marketing system, very simply, is a process created so that somebody can look at your business step-by-step, and at the end of the process they will be in a place where they will either be able to say yes or no to your business.

In the end, people will join your business because of *you*. They know you, they trust you, and they like you. So don't think you have to be a salesman or a pitch artist. The system is in place just to give people an understanding of a way to do the business. The system is important because if you use it properly, the people that join you will do the same thing you do. Even if you've got an incredible circle of influence, use your company's system adamantly, not your own ability to influence.

Typically, the systems in our industry are simple. You basically call somebody, offer your opportunity to them in a way that they'll know you, like you, and trust you right away, and then direct them to a tool, like a Web site or a recorded conference call. Literally walk them to that point, let them evaluate what they see and hear, and book a time to call them back. When you call them back, it's a good idea to have somebody else involved in the conversation who has a little more experience and success than you do. Even if you are somebody who's making $20,000 a month in the industry, don't deviate from this. Use somebody else to validate what you're talking about.

Third-party credibility is vitally important. Before they join, every single person that I introduce to my company will talk to three or four people – third parties that they haven't met before. Have you ever given somebody financial advice based on your own experience because you want to assist them, and they think you're crazy and never take your advice? And then they'll take the very same advice from the insurance salesman they just paid for that information three months later. People like to have information validated by a source they don't know; this is just human nature. So one of the most important parts of a successful system is getting a third party to validate your information.

Create Passion

Now that you've set up your office, created your list, and you understand your system, you're ready to create some passion. Become familiar with your products and services. Understand your products intimately and use them – become a product of your products. If you don't have a personal story to share about your product or service, how do you expect somebody else to get passionate about it and want to follow you in your business?

The biggest thing I can tell you is to become a student. Become a student of your business. Leaders are readers, and readers are leaders. Pick up a great book, and learn all you can about the network marketing industry. It's a massive industry, and we all should to become experts on it. Some excellent books are *The New Professionals: The Rise of Network Marketing; Your First Year in Network Marketing; Good to Great;* and *How to Win Friends and Influence People.* You can find these books on Amazon or at your local library. Start reading one of them today. Become a passionate leader yourself.

Logs, Journals, and Agendas Will Save Your Life

Anyone who knows me will be the first to tell you that I have developed a keen ability to handle many different tasks simultaneously, to multitask. It actually drives my assistant crazy. Have you ever known a true multitasker and wondered how they ever manage to keep it all straight?

Greg Fullerton is one of the original founders of the time management giant, FranklinCovey. Based in Salt Lake City, Utah, FranklinCovey boasts over a billion dollars a year in the time management arena. They are the world leaders. Greg is one of the most organized and efficient people I have ever met. Obviously, he keeps his entire life in a Franklin Planner. Greg is also one of the founders of the network marketing company I'm with. When I first started to work with my company, I was able to spend a bit of time with him, and he walked me through how he organizes his life with the planner. His strategy is so simple and so powerful.

As I listened to Greg, I looked back at my own life and the lives of the seven inspirational leaders that I studied, and I realized that it all comes down to organization. While Greg plans his entire life out in a Franklin Planner, I use a PDA (an iPhone) and a notepad to keep on track. Each of the seven leaders had their own systems to stay organized.

Anyone in the world can become organized. If you want to become a millionaire in our industry, then you absolutely have to work on attention to detail and multitasking.

My Secret

I keep track of all my appointments and contacts in my iPhone. I also carry a simple white steno pad with me everywhere I go. At the start of every day, I take ten minutes to get organized. I open the steno pad to a clean page. On the top section of the spiral metal spine, I write the names and numbers of everyone that I have to call that day, along with a brief explanation of the details. On the bottom of the page, I write a list of the tasks that I plan to accomplish that day. As I go through the day, I check off the things that I accomplish and add anything that comes up to the existing lists. The next day I start over by compiling new lists and carrying forward anything pertinent from the day before.

Here's another other important point. Every great leader I can think of has one thing in common. They take ten or fifteen minutes every morning to collect themselves for the day. When I realized this and adapted it, life became clear and focused. In that ten minutes, they review the day before, prioritize their outstanding tasks, and read a few pages from a good book.

As you become more successful, you'll become busier; it comes with the territory. If you wait until you are successful to get organized, you will never become successful. Start today by developing your own system of time management. I strongly suggest that you start with FranklinCovey's system. Over a billion dollars per year must mean something! Regardless of what system you use, use something. We're simply not meant to hold everything in our heads.

If the greatest leaders in the world use agendas, logs, and journals, shouldn't you?

You can now breathe a sigh of relief to know that these leaders are not superhuman – they are just meticulous. They use time management tools and techniques to become detailed-oriented and multitaskers. You can, too!

How to Become More Detail-Oriented

1. Keep a list.
2. Prioritize each item on your list.
3. When you start a task, finish a task.
4. Take the first ten minutes of every day to get organized and create your day's task list.
5. Use an agenda or PDA.
6. Spend twenty minutes every day reading a good book.
7. When you are with someone, make it a point to notice personal details.
8. Keep a follow-up journal related to your business.

10

Create a Gravitational Pull

"Conscious of the power of connection, the best leaders take responsibility for relating with others on a regular basis."
JOHN C. MAXWELL

Network marketing is a simple business of talking to people. Go out and tell as many people as you can about your business as fast as possible. In this chapter, I'll share the mindset that I use to create gravitational pull, and I'll show you how to attract people by creating your own gravitational pull.

Understanding gravitational pull has had the biggest impact on turning my life around after the Christmas that my leaders confronted me and left the business. I realized that the inspirational leaders I studied had this ability to attract others, and I knew if I wanted to get better, I required it. This is the one area of change that I have focused the most attention on, and it has had the biggest impact on my success. The great part is that you can learn it; you can gain it. I have put together some simple techniques that, if you practice them, will make your gravitational pull go through the roof. More people will like you than ever before. If more people like you, then they'll start to trust you more, and your prospecting ability will hit the stratosphere – and when it does, your ability to prospect will become second nature.

What Is Gravitational Pull?

Gravitational pull is the ability to capture the attention of another person. It's the natural (or practiced, as in my case) ability to grab another person's interest. Gravitational pull is that attraction that some people seem to have when they walk in a room. This is the person who walks into a room at a social event, and everyone notices him or her. Even walking through a crowd, not saying a word, people just seem to gravitate towards people like this. Most top leaders in network marketing have this type of force field around them that spontaneously draws other people towards them.

Every one of the seven leaders I studied had this magnetic quality. It wasn't forced; instead, it was amazingly natural. Mother Teresa just quietly walking down a street would have thousands of people flocking to her, even before she was a household name. She was quiet and unassuming, but her interior gravitational pull was incredibly strong and attractive.

John F. Kennedy also had a strong gravitational pull; he was the epitome of charisma. He knew how to project himself into the hearts of the American people. Gandhi possessed this quality as well. All of the inspirational leaders I studied were recognized as leaders in large part because of their tremendous ability to influence others and their appealing mystique. They were fascinating individuals who continue to be intriguing to the rest of us. I'm still learning about them – there's always more to learn about the secrets of success and personal strength they possess.

As I seriously focused on becoming a better person, I noticed something happening – it seemed that I always had people that wanted to be around me. Suddenly I never, ever lacked for somebody to go to dinner with. This was a huge difference, because three years earlier, literally *nobody* wanted to be around me.

A Book that Changed My Life

Last July I traveled to Asia for five weeks, where I visited five different countries to speak about network marketing. Hong Kong is the longest leg of the flight, and I always fly first class because on the plane they have these incredible new pod seats that are almost like little rooms. The seat rolls out flat into a bed, a canopy comes over the top, and you can effectively shut out the world. On this particular trip, just before I boarded the plane I went into a store at the airport to buy a bottle of water, and at the cash register the title of a book just jumped out of me: *How to Make People Like You in 90 Seconds or Less*.

I bought the book, threw it in my bag, and headed for the plane. Anything you can do to get people to like you better is important, because as you've learned in this book, people only join the business for three reasons – they know you, **they like you**, and they trust you. The plane took off, and I discovered that my reclining seat didn't work. So there I was, beginning a fifteen-hour flight to Hong Kong, my seat is broken, and there wasn't another empty seat on the plane to move to.

To make matters worse, my individual personal entertainment center didn't work either – no movies, no music. Out of desperation, I started flipping through *How to Make People Like You in 90 Seconds or Less*, and instantly I was blown away by how this book spoke to me. It was the essence of everything that I'd ever learned about gravitational pull. The author, Nicholas Boothman, reveals the secret of how you get people to like you in literally ninety seconds or less. I read this book *four times* on the way to Hong Kong. In approximately 185 pages, it covered all the essentials of building rapport with people and learning how to connect with them.

Over the next three weeks as I traveled around Asia, I was on fourteen airplanes, and on each flight I just kept reading this book over and over again. When I got back to my office, I put the book on my assistant's desk and told her, "Wendy, you need to find this author. I don't care if he lives in Milan or New York City, I want to go and meet him. Get me an appointment with him." I wanted to get to know this guy!

As so often happens, the universe is there to assist us. A few hours later, my assistant came back to me, giggling and saying, "Well, you won't need a plane ticket. Nicholas Boothman lives twenty minutes down the road from your house!" The irony is that he spent twenty-five years in international photojournalism. He was a top advertising photographer in the fashion industry, traveling to Milan and Rome and Portugal and New York City, so for him to be living down the road from me in Canada was just unbelievable.

Since Nick lives nearby, we've had the opportunity to spend time together, and we've become good friends. The concepts that Nick teaches on how to get people to like you and the pitfalls he shares about how to avoid the not liking you are directly in line with everything I've learned about not offending people.

How I Created Gravitational Pull

At the end of that first year when my leaders confronted me and told me what an evil person I had become, at first I was really confused. Up until then, I always had received pretty decent feedback about being able to make great first impressions. However, I came to the realization that my problem wasn't so much the first impression; it was the lasting impression, how I dealt with people over the long-term. Over time I have learned to treat people the way I am able to treat them in those first couple of minutes after meeting them.

I've learned to stay consistent with the way I treated people in the first ninety seconds.

Something I notice when I look at any of the seven inspirational leaders, as well as Greg, Steve, and Fred (the owners of my current company), is that they all have an amazing natural ability to get other people to like them. I think this quality, more than almost any other, is really tied to their success. It's that certain *je ne sais quoi*. When they walk into a room, maybe it's their smile, maybe it's the way they're dressed, but somehow these leaders always seem to grab people's attention. When they're involved in conversations, there are certain little things about them that make people want to be around them. As I studied those inspirational leaders, I came to the conclusion that part of their success came from their ability to quickly build relationships with people – not here and there, but consistently over time. It was part of who they were.

In my own life, I had the ability to get people to like me quickly, but I was terrible at keeping that positive connection. A friend pointed out to me that I had the uncanny ability to create a friendship with somebody and then ruin that friendship within the first fifteen minutes. I guess I never really thought a lot about people; I had to come to the realization that I didn't really care very much others. By studying the seven leaders and observing how charismatic they were and how skilled they were at building relationships, I finally realized what an important quality this was.

I knew that if I was going to be the leader that I wanted to be – an inspirational leader, a truly great leader – I had to create this same all-encompassing gravitational pull in myself. I understood the basics of this, but I had not yet developed the focus or the ability to build and sustain lasting relationships. This was a really tough challenge for me.

I went back to one of my friends, one of those first five guys that I talked to, and I began to rebuild my friendship with him. In the process, I said to him, "You know, all the leaders I studied had this incredible gravitational pull. People just naturally wanted to be around them." I asked him to think about me and give me some points that I could work on if I wanted to enhance this in myself. Together we put together an essential list of key things to draw people to me and create this gravitational pull. I live by this list today; it's a list of very simple things, but I apply them to every interaction I have.

Keys to Connecting with Others

First, I make eye contact with as many people as I can. The first time I make eye contact with someone, I always smile. In the beginning, this was really hard for me to do. Remember, I had a policeman's personality. Whenever I looked at somebody before, I would automatically think the worst of them; it was simply ingrained in me. But now I play a little mindset game with myself. Whenever I see somebody new, in my mind I say, "That's a great person; I want to be their friend." When I say that, my heart lightens up, my eyes soften, and I spontaneously smile at them. I don't smile at them as if I'm a two-bit car salesperson trying to sell them a used clunker; I just flash them a gentle smile, showing a bit of teeth, and I look them right in the eye. I'm really saying, "Hi, how are you doing?" with my eyes and my smile. And any time I have the opportunity, I always introduce myself and extend my hand in a handshake as soon as possible.

Whenever I shake someone's hand, I'm always very cautious about that handshake because it's such an important part of creating gravitational pull. When some people shake your hand, they nearly squeeze the blood right out you. You feel like they're going to rip your hand right off. Then there's the other extreme: people with what I call a "wet noodle" handshake. What you want to achieve is a perfect interaction with somebody else through the combination of your eyes, smile, introduction, and handshake. That first handshake is very important overall for the beginnings of a long-term relationship.

People with gravitational pull are very charismatic. When they meet someone, you observe them looking directly into that person's eyes. You see their gentle smile. You see that open-handed handshake, that perfect grip. Whenever they are with you, they are really with you.

This was something I had to learn to develop. In the past, whenever I was talking to somebody, my mind was clearly elsewhere. This is something that my friends pointed out to me as one of my biggest flaws. I came to see how counterproductive this was. There I was, trying to build a relationship with somebody, but because my mind was somewhere else, they would automatically conclude that I didn't really want to be around them. When I thought about this, I realized that I would have interpreted it exactly the same way.

Now I live by the adage that when I'm with somebody, I'm really *with them*. It doesn't matter what else is going on in my life. When I'm communicating with somebody, I block everything else out. The top leaders in the world all have this natural ability to block out the rest of the world when they're talking with someone.

One of my mentors said that a millionaire in network marketing is somebody that has a million friends. That was a profound statement for me, because I had to face into the fact that I never really cared about being with anyone. Another one of my mentors, Michael Clouse, taught me that people are only going to join the business if they know you, like you, and trust you. What can you take away from these two keys? Well, if you want to make a million dollars in network marketing, you have to make more friends. The only way you can make more friends is if people like you. If they like you and they're your friends, they're more likely to join your business. And the easiest way in the world to create friends is to actively be interested in others.

Part of my own personal development process was realizing that I truly *did* like people, and I really did want them to like me. All key leaders take an active interest in the people around them. Whenever I get to know someone now, I ask open-ended questions about their life as a tool to engage them in conversation. I ask questions about their family, their occupation, what they like to do for recreation, etc. What I'm really looking for is the one thing that's more important to them than anything else. I really want to get to know them. I want to have a relationship with everybody that I meet.

My goal is to make a million friends! The fastest way to do that is to get people to talk, get them to open up. The more I did this, the more I discovered that people love to talk about themselves. As I developed a strong gravitational pull, I learned to speak less and say more. I became skilled at asking open-ended questions and letting others talk.

I learned that it's very important to *never* interrupt anybody. In the past, I had this incredibly bad habit: whenever I'd ask somebody a question, in the middle of their answer I would inevitably interrupt them. Right in the middle of a comment, I'd jump in to get *my* point across. I didn't see this as a bad habit – I just thought I had a lot of value to add, and I couldn't wait for them to finish. I was very impatient with people. I offended people, and I never knew why.

It's so easy to offend people if you interrupt them. True leaders always wait until a person is finished talking, regardless of what they're saying. They honor the person by doing this. If you interrupt somebody, you dishonor that person. I'm sure you know somebody who is exactly like I used to be. I'm hoping you'll give this book to them so they can read it themselves. Maybe it will open their eyes.

If you are the type of person that interrupts others during conversation, you're just hurting yourself. You'll never get people to like you, and you'll have a hard time getting a response from people in your business. Maybe you're saying, "Oh, my gosh – that's me!" That's what happened to me. I realized that this was one of the biggest problems I had; it was one of the reasons so many people disliked me. I realized that none of leaders I studied were like this.

Details, Details

There are many small pieces to creating stronger relationships more quickly. How you look is important. What you wear is important. In my case, I decided to hire a professional shopper to assist me with creating a wardrobe that worked.

How you smell is also important. Have you ever met somebody who has halitosis? Some people have this issue and don't realize it. The smallest details of how you come across to somebody else will affect your ability to build a relationship.

Be cognizant of other people's space; respect the three-foot rule. I've known some people who would get two inches from my face and start talking. People like this have no idea how offensive this is to 90 percent of the population.

I've had the opportunity to travel to twenty-five countries around the world, and I've realized that the customs in each country are very diverse. The way we interact with each other in North America can be quite offensive to somebody in India or Indonesia. When you're traveling overseas, learn to be aware of the customs of each country you visit and interact with people accordingly. All great leaders have professional people – publicists and stylists – that get them ready to interact with people from other cultures. You can learn to be aware of these things too. You don't need a professional publicist to assist you – if you are traveling abroad, go to the Web site of that country and look up "customs and protocols." You will find everything you need to know about what to do – and, more importantly, what *not* to do – to create better gravitational pull.

Every piece of the puzzle, no matter how small, matters. When I started learning about gravitational pull, I applied all of these things to my life. Now when I interact with somebody, I'm fully with them, no matter what else is going on in my life. I always start with a gentle smile and an open handshake. I tell them who I am, and I ask open-ended questions. I've learned to be patient with people, and I've discovered that I truly enjoy and care about them.

Over the last four years, the number one thing that I focus on improving most often is my habit of interrupting people. I'm automatically conscious of this tendency all the time. I'm also aware of my appearance. I always take a look at myself before I go into public to make sure that I don't have any hairs out of place, my teeth are clean, and my clothes are proper and neat. I'm acutely aware of this stuff, because I want to have the right impact on people. There's an old saying, "You don't get a second chance to make a first impression." First impressions are key.

Create Your Own Gravitational Pull

If you want to be successful in life, forget about network marketing. Instead, focus on creating your own gravitational pull. Once you know what gravitational pull is, you can learn to create it, and then you can learn to maintain it, making it an integral part of who you are.

Create a Gravitational Pull

In many ways, creating gravitational pull starts with your appearance. You've got to strive to look your best. This is *not* about vanity or appearances for appearance sake. Looking good feels good, and when you feel good, others are drawn to you.

You may say, "Well, people just have to accept me the way I am." There's no problem with this as long as you can accept who you are. If you're happy with the success you've had in life, if you're happy with what you're getting out of life right now, that's great, but in my world there's nothing wrong with trying to become a better person and creating gravitational pull.

Frankly, I think everybody should make sure they appear at their best all the time. If you want to create great gravitational pull, as shallow as this may sound, people are attracted to people that feel good and look good. It's not about how much you weigh or whether you were blessed with model good looks; it's an overall positive feeling someone receives from their first contact with you.

If you're really serious about increasing your gravitational pull, do what I did. Take a serious interest in looking the best you can, both with your own physical appearance and how you dress. True leaders dress impeccably – they make a conscious effort to look their best. In order to do this, you must first respect and value yourself, and this becomes the foundation that allows you to extend that to other people.

Always dress with the styles of the day. You don't have to drop thousands of dollars on clothes, but if your wardrobe is full of bright green paisley shirts, they're not going to help you to increase gravitational pull, unless it's still 1972! How you look *is* important.

Next, how you approach someone is important. Make eye contact, have a firm (not crushing, not limp) handshake. Be aware of your tone of voice. It's very important to slow down when you speak. Make your voice welcoming and inviting. Be precise with your words. These are all areas for continual improvement. All the leaders I studied made personal development an ongoing priority.

Nick Boothman's book, *How to Make People Like You in 90 Seconds or Less*, is the bible of gravitational pull. I first coined the term "gravitational pull" years before I read this book, but Nick put it all into perspective for me. In fact, if I'd have read Nick Boothman's book first, I might not have ever developed the term gravitational pull. It's appearance. It's eye contact. It's how you shake somebody's hand. If you're in a foreign country, it's understanding the customs of that country so you don't offend someone.

Gravitational pull is about honestly wanting to get to know somebody. When you're with someone, really *be* with that person. Ask people open-ended questions, and then let them respond. It all works together. If you create a really strong gravitational pull, people will like you more. If they like you more, they'll be more inclined to join your business.

Dealing with Your New Gravitational Pull

As you begin to develop a great gravitational pull, suddenly many people will want to be around you and hang out with you and spend time with you and get to know you better – and you won't be used to this at all. You may begin to feel a little overwhelmed or put undue pressure on yourself to perform in this situation. How do you deal with it?

My advice is to stay real. When your gravitational pull starts to increase, just be yourself and continue to be real. Always have respect for yourself in the process. Retain sufficient time for yourself. When you have that type of gravitational pull, you're going to require time to unwind. I often like to spend quiet time with my family, and I recognize that this is vitally important.

When you have lots of people around you all the time, it's important to fulfill your commitments – every single one of them. Make sure that you develop an attitude of gratitude. Your modus operandi should be to always under promise and over deliver. Don't say anything that you're not going to live up to. When you develop huge gravitational pull, you want to be very cognizant of how and what you say to other people, and be careful to say things that empower others.

What if you're a Type A personality like me who has a tendency to be a bit impatient with others? How can you slow down, become more patient, and become more effective in your communications? As a police officer, I had a tendency to be demanding, controlling, impatient – in a lot of cases, lives depended on me being this way. Those qualities were strongly ingrained in me. But how can you create a strong sense of gravitational pull if you are completely impatient?

It's all about developing the right mindset. You have to realize that your standards will be higher than those around you. You must apply your standards to yourself, while at the same time letting everybody else be who they are. Learn to let things go. Understand that often other people will let you down, and you have to just let it roll off your back like water off a duck's back, as the saying goes. Accept people for who they are, and understand that their strengths may not be the same as yours.

Remember, Rome wasn't built in a day. I speak from experience; learning patience has been one of the biggest challenges I've ever had in my life. I want everything yesterday. I know that I can move at a million miles an hour, but most people around me can't, or they don't want to. This has caused me to become very critical of some people and very impatient with others. I still have my moments; I'm not perfect. But I've become so much more aware of the fact that we have to love and respect everybody for who they are. It's really important to stay even-keeled and patient – with yourself first of all.

There's tremendous power in developing your own unique gravitational pull. With it comes the responsibility to use it wisely to serve others – a topic we'll cover in the next chapter.

Simple Steps to Increasing Gravitational Pull

1. Read *How to Make People Like You in 90 Seconds or Less* by Nicholas Boothman.
2. Always try your best to look your best.
3. Work on truly listening to others.
4. Avoid others' personal space.
5. Ask open-ended relationship-building questions.
6. When you're with someone, really be with them.
7. Be sincerely interested in others.
8. Do not interrupt at all costs.
9. Smile and introduce yourself all the time.
10. Create a goal to make two new friends every day.

11

Serve Others

"In this life we cannot do great things. We can only do small things with great love."
MOTHER TERESA OF CALCUTTA

Robert Macauley is the founder of AmeriCares, a relief organization that distributes critical medicines and medical supplies to the world's poor in times of disaster. He's often been in the position of raising money for his organization himself, and he credits Mother Teresa with teaching him how to be a beggar. "I learned from the best!" he said in a *Guideposts* article (*Mother T & Me*, *Guideposts*, April 1, 2006).

He and Mother Teresa had visited several orphanages in Guatamala and were flying to Mexico. This is where his lesson on begging took place. When the stewardess brought the food (this was back in the day when you actually got a meal on a flight), Mother Teresa spoke up. She asked the stewardess how much the meal would cost in U.S. dollars. "About a dollar," came the answer. Then Mother Teresa asked if she could she have a dollar for the poor if she gave the meal back. The startled stewardess went to consult with the pilot, returning a few minutes later with the news. "Yes, Mother," she said, "You may have the money for the poor."

Mother Teresa handed over her tray. Bob Macauley felt compelled to hand his over as well, as there was no way he could eat in front of her now. Suddenly people across the aisle began handing in their trays too. Finally the flight attendant said over the loud speaker that for anyone who gave up their meal, the airlines would donate a dollar to the poor. In the end, the entire plane (129 passengers) gave up their meals, including the crew.

But Mother Teresa wasn't finished. She then asked if the airlines would give her all the meals. She knew that they couldn't be reused, and she wanted to give them to the poor. This request was graciously granted – but then what? How to transport these meals? Mother Teresa had one more request: Could the airlines allow her to use one of their trucks? Amazingly, this too was granted, and off she went to a poor section of Mexico City. Swarms of hungry children gathered around that truck, eager for the meals she began handing out.

On the way back to the airport, Mother Teresa explained to Bob Macauley, "It's easy to ask when you're doing it for the poor!"

We All Think of Philanthropy Someday...

When I really started to study the seven leaders that I profiled earlier in the book, it didn't surprise me at all that they were all incredible givers. Obviously, Gandhi and Mother Teresa gave their entire lives, but this may not be so obvious with business leaders. However, did you know that Bill Gates is one of the biggest givers (philanthropists) in the world today? Mr. Gates' charitable foundations give millions of dollars every year to a whole host of good causes. Wouldn't *you* like to be a philanthropist? Haven't we all thought at one time or another about giving? Unfortunately for most of us, as soon as the thought enters our minds, it is quickly replaced with negative thoughts of the bills that are adding up, the mortgage payments that are due, the educations that need to be paid for, and our philanthropic thoughts are put on hold.

The more I studied inspirational leaders, the more I realized that service to others was ingrained in their souls. I wanted so desperately to become a better person that I started to really devote time to thinking about how I could serve others. While collecting my thoughts, I realized that service to others is not about how much money you can give to your favorite charity; it is much deeper and much simpler than that.

Back in 2003 and 2004, I treated people terribly. I was condescending, even belligerent in some cases, and definitely critical of other people all the time. Thinking back on that time, I realized that I wasn't serving others. Serving others in its simplest, most powerful form is how you treat people every day. How you make people feel on a daily basis forms the basis for service to others.

If you want to be a great Bill Gates-like philanthropist tomorrow, then you have to respect others more than you respect yourself today. You need to wake up every morning and begin every day by asking yourself, "Who can I make feel good about themselves today?" People do not become philanthropists automatically; they grow into this. If you take a look back through Bill Gates' life, he has always been a caring, loving, giving person. There are clues through his entire life that he went out of his way to do things for others. Most times in the early days, it was random acts of kindness, politeness, and innocent acts, but it was all serving in nature.

Where Service to Others Really Begins

As I started to really understand where service to others actually starts, I became really excited. I realized that by focusing on gravitational pull, I was simultaneously serving others. I was doing what great leaders do! This was awesome for me because I was "killing two birds with one stone." Sorry for the bad analogy, but you get my point. I'm still aggressive and want as much as possible today, so if I can tackle two traits at the same time, I'm excited.

Here's the deal. In the last chapter, we talked about increasing your attraction to other people by getting them to like you, being sincerely interested in them, and making them feel good when you are around them. Well, if you do these things, aren't you simultaneously serving them? You are making them feel good about themselves. Let's say that prior to your interaction with a person, he or she is having a bad day, and then you come up and greet them with a welcoming smile, a calm gesture, and then you follow up with an sincere interest in them. In minutes you will "turn that frown upside down." You will bring that person back to a great place. You will be SERVING THEM!

Try it – go up to a person and practice what you learned together in the last chapter, and watch how you serve them and bring them into a good space. Isn't this cool? We're multitasking our personality enhancement. This is AWESOME!

The greatest form of service to others is simple everyday courtesy. You have to be courteous. Don't be afraid to open a door for someone. If some sneezes, say, "Bless you." If there is only one cookie left on the plate, offer it to another person. These little simple courtesies go a long way.

Random Acts of Kindness

On a recent business trip, the plane was grounded for mechanical difficulties. There were three people working as part of the ground crew for the national airline that I was flying, and over the course of nine hours, they were bombarded by the 200 people that were constantly being aggressive with them, blaming them for everything that was going on. I could feel the intensity of that angry mom who wasn't going to get home in time for her child's birthday party and who chose to take that out on the airline employee behind the counter. Or that twenty-three-year-old just coming back from Cancun, Mexico, still tired from a week of partying and expressing her frustration. Or the profane man from the Midwest who couldn't think of anything more productive to do than to swear at the lady behind the counter.

By the end of the day, these women were beaten down. It wasn't their fault that the plane broke down. And quite frankly, I'm happy that the pilot made the decision to keep us on the ground and potentially save our lives, but others didn't see it that way. I could see that these three women were shattered by the end of that long day, and then around 9:00 p.m., I came up with an idea. I ran through the airport for about forty-five minutes as the stores were closing until I found what I was looking for. I purchased a little package, ran back to these ladies behind the counter – they were gone. I chased them down. I searched the airport until I found the crew room for this national airline carrier. I opened the door... I didn't know their names... I pulled from behind my back three bouquets of beautiful summer flowers. I gave one bouquet to each of the women, and I said, "Ladies, I'm sorry for what you've gone through today. I truly want to thank you for everything you've done. I don't know your names, and you don't know mine, but I just want you to know that there are people out there that are grateful for what you're doing."

Why am I telling you this? What does this have to do with network marketing? I'm sharing this story with you because things like this fill your heart with the power and the passion of people, and if you're willing to do little things every day, you'll be strengthening those serving muscles and adding to your own life. Don't be afraid to compliment that new person you've just introduced to your business. Make people feel important. Why? Because they truly are!

The people in your business will become your best friends; they are your allies. These are the people you want to spend the rest of your life with, so make sure that they know how valuable they are to you. Do things every day to increase your own life – to increase the betterment of other people – and I guarantee you you'll have a strong, successful business for life.

Put Others First

You absolutely have to like people to be in this industry. You have to be willing to do things for others before yourself. Now, make no mistake about it – your goal is to be successful. You're no good to anybody unless you're feeling successful yourself. But one of the ways to achieve the ultimate success is to focus on other people and serve them. There is nothing better in this world than making other people happy.

If I can give you one piece of advice that's more important than anything else I've shared in this book, it's this: If you want to build a big business, and you want to do it right, you have to love people. Go out there every day and serve others. Before you go to bed every night, hug your wife, kiss your kids, put a smile on somebody's face. Random acts of kindness are powerful. They're good for your heart; they're good for other people's hearts.

On my return flight from another business trip, I had a great conversation with a person from Atlantic Canada named Bernie who was sitting next to me. We had a wonderful time together. As we started talking, I asked him questions about himself; I sincerely wanted to know because he seemed like a great person. He told me he was a guidance counselor and that he had spent most of his life empowering and teaching others to want more. He talked about goal setting – helping and encouraging individuals to reach for what they want, never saying no and never giving up. I walked away with his phone number – a new friend in Atlantic Canada, and of course, a new opportunity to introduce somebody to this business. I just don't stop. Why? Because I love people! If you truly love people, you will never stop talking about your business.

Give a Few Hours of Every Week to a Good Cause

It really doesn't matter where you're at in your life; someone needs your assistance. If you really want to become a great servant to others, start today. My family and I have decided to volunteer a couple of hours a week in our community. We're going to decide how over the Christmas break. We've realized that in spite of our busy lives, social calendars, etc., we need to give back to our community. You can do the same thing. Look around your community, find a good charitable cause that feels right in your heart, and get in there and help. This will assist you to meet new people in the process, you'll create new friendships, and you know what will happen next – people will know you, like you, and trust you….

How to Start Serving Others

- Serve other by increasing your gravitational pull.
- Do not interrupt others.
- Be respectful of others.
- Engage in random acts of kindness, the simpler the better.
- Decide to be a philanthropist, and realize that you have to grow into one.
- Take time for your family.
- Give a few hours every week to a good cause.

12

Live in the Now

"Declare today that you are blessed with creativity, courage, talent, and abundance. You are blessed with a strong will, self-control, and self-discipline.... You are blessed with a compassionate heart and a positive outlook. Declare that everything you put your hand to is going to prosper and succeed. Declare it today and every day!"
JOEL OSTEEN

My journey really began to change when I started to understand and appreciate gratitude and find meaning in the small elements of life, not just in the huge goals and targets and results that I hoped to create.

Joel Osteen ends his best-selling book, *Becoming a Better You*, with the advice to be happy now, and he reminds us that this is a choice. On your journey to achieving big goals, it is an important choice to be happy and fully present to your life *now*.

The Pitfalls of Multitasking

I've always had many, many things going on in my life at the same time. When I was a police detective, at one time I ran two different companies at the same time. I've always been involved in social groups with my kids and with my network marketing business, and I've always enjoyed many different relationships with lots of different people. I'm cursed with the kind of mind that has a thousand things going on at the same time.

What I've realized, though, is that even though I'm able to multitask, it hasn't served me, because whenever I was with somebody, I was never really with them. Many of my friends are going to read this book, and they'll knowing *exactly* what I'm talking about because they've been through it with me. Regardless of what you've got going on in your life, when you're with somebody, it's essential to be with that person fully – body, mind, and soul.

Do yourself a favor and watch some videos of Mother Teresa and Mahatma Gandhi and notice how they interacted with people. You'll see that they were intensely centered on the people they were with. They paid attention to what was being said, they really listened, and they were able to process what they heard.

When you're with someone and you can't remember the details of the conversation, this is a clue that you're not living in the now. That's exactly what used to happen to me, but now when I'm with people, I literally focus on the words they're saying, how they're expressing themselves, and what they're seeking to communicate.

What's Truly Important?

So many people focus on trying to get to that pot of gold, and then, when they get there the pot is empty. The gold was actually right there in the individual experiences, the joys that they lived with people along the way – their family, their children, their business associates, etc.

There are many stories of people who go through life, working so hard to achieve some goal they thought was meaningful, only to realize that while they were busy achieving monetary rewards, their relationships, their health, and their spiritual life suffered, and in the end they found themselves empty and lost, even in the midst of financial wealth and career advancement. How many marriages that have fallen apart because one of the spouses was driven to obtain and achieve and become more and more, all the while thinking they were creating a better life for their family? By the time they reached their goal, their family was gone.

The secret lies in enjoying the journey, each and every bump along the way, and not losing sight of what's truly important. Every one of the inspirational leaders learned this lesson. I've read many stories about Kennedy. In spite of how busy he was in running the country, he always took time for his young family, especially his son and daughter. Both John F. Kennedy Jr. and his older sister Caroline helped create the impression of an ideal family living in the White House. There are many photos showing Kennedy playing with his children, and his love for them has become a lasting part of his legacy.

At Pierre Trudeau's funeral, his son told the story of how his dad took time to create a special memory for him. When Trudeau's son was about six years old, he went on his first "official" trip – he went with Trudeau and his grandfather to the North Pole. His son said that, for him, the best thing about the trip was spending lots of time with his dad, because normally Trudeau was always working.

They reached Alert, Canada's northernmost point. Trudeau's son began to be a little bored, because somehow Trudeau still had lots of work to do. But then one "frozen, windswept Arctic afternoon," Trudeau bundled his son up, put him in a jeep, and took him on a "special, top-secret mission." They drove slowly past many gray buildings, finally turning a corner and stopping in front of a red building. Trudeau's son jumped out of the jeep and ran towards the door, but he was told to look in the window instead.

As he peered into the frost-covered window, in the gloomy half-light, he could just make out a figure hunched over a cluttered worktable... he was wearing a red suit trimmed with white fur! Trudeau's son said, "And that's when I understood just how powerful and wonderful my father was."

Lessons from My Early Network Marketing Days

My daughter Laura was born one month before I joined my first network marketing company. I went nuts with my business right away. I was just enthralled by the potential I saw. Two years into the journey was when it first hit me: I realized that I had pretty much missed most of my daughter's first two years of life. I remember very few details about her at age one or at age two. It's sad; those years can never be relived. Many of you reading this book know exactly what I'm talking about. This is truly one of the most painful parts of my life today. I am sitting in the Denver airport right now, editing this chapter. As I read this paragraph about missing my daughter's first two years, I burst into tears. I am having a hard time seeing the keyboard right now through my tears. I have been gone for twelve days. During those past twelve days, I have been in Philippines, Indonesia, Singapore, and Utah, and now eight days before Christmas I am finally on my way home. I cannot wait to hug Julie and the kids later today!

For instance, I remember when we were getting ready to celebrate Laura's first birthday. I was so focused on building my network business that I had decided to work in Calgary, Alberta for the month, prospecting and working with my reps in that area. I missed my daughter's birthday because I was in Calgary, and it's one of the biggest regrets of my life. Luckily, Laura doesn't remember that. But I do. I made a conscious effort to be more involved in my

family after this realization.

There's a song called *Cat's in the Cradle* by Cat Stevens that conveys this very message – that looking back you realize all too late that you'd like to be able to go back and do things differently. One of my friends, Craig Case, always cites this song when he speaks to a crowd. The words are chilling to me. Every time I hear that song I cry, thinking about my first couple years in network marketing and how I missed being involved in my kids' lives. It reminds me to stay grounded.

Everyone that is building a network marketing business or any other kind of entrepreneurial endeavor ought to realize that the journey itself is the most important part of the process. If you're going to be successful in life, if you're going to be a true inspirational leader, you have to design your life so that you create time for what is most important to you – your family. Inspirational leaders all achieve this, and they're busier than any of us; they accomplish more than most of us will ever hope to.

Many people who are attempting to build a network marketing business are extremely driven. They see the opportunity; they grab it by both hands, and they begin going for it to the exclusion of all else that's going on in their life, and it creates a huge imbalance. In my own life, I sacrificed everything during my first two years in network marketing, after I quit my job as a cop. I blocked everything else out. I was blinded by my desire to be successful in this industry. The money that I was making just made it worse because I saw the bigger numbers. I literally can't tell you how much I regret this. If I could do it all over again, I would approach my business very differently right from the start.

Schedule Time for What Is Most Important

After realizing how much of my children's lives I had already missed, I decided to live by a schedule. On that schedule, I block out time for my family. I live by an agenda, and it's right there: four nights a week, dinner with the family. I have time in my agenda allotted for my kids and for my wife. Friday night I shut the phone off, and my wife and I enjoy some time together after the kids go to bed. Most of the time we just stay at home and talk. Once in a while we get a sitter and go out for dinner. Either way, it's our time together – no matter what.

I have to keep reminding myself every day that what's truly important is the here and now, because I'm such a huge goal-driven person. Because of my newfound awareness, I take more vacations with my family on a regular basis now than I ever did before, and guess what? My business hasn't suffered at all!

Your ability to stay organized and focused and to create time in your schedule for your family will be directly related to your success in network marketing. I've known way too many people that wanted to be so successful in network marketing that they blocked out their family and friends, their husbands, their wives, their kids, everything. And that blind desire to be successful in network marketing destroyed their families.

Success in network marketing doesn't require this. It is as simple as having an agenda and jotting time slots into it every single week for your family. It's not about the *quantity* of time; what's important is the *quality*. It's making sure that you don't forget about what is most important to you. Remember, you got started in network marketing to create a better life for your family. You have to design your life every day to include time for your family now; otherwise when you do become successful, you'll have forgotten how to spend time with your family, and you'll be disconnected with who they have become.

Some network marketers use this as an excuse. They procrastinate and use their families as the excuse to keep from producing. These individuals would do well to take a long, hard look in the mirror. They have never crossed over into action, and so they remain unsuccessful. Eventually something might come along that will force them to get moving. Procrastinating creates a tremendous amount of guilt. If this is something you struggle with, you can expedite the process by just *deciding*. The sooner you choose action, the better off you are. (We'll be covering this in the next chapter.)

There are two sides to the pendulum. There's the person who's going too fast with their blinders on, so focused on that one goal that they miss everything else going on around them. That's not being present. Then there's the other person that's so distracted by everything else that's going on around them that they can't ever focus on their goal, and that's not being present either.

The Solution

The way to stay present to your life while you are building for the future is to make sure that your future goals are balanced within the context of your whole life. You want to make sure you take time for yourself and your health. You don't want to neglect your family – the very ones you want to create a better life for. Block out on your agenda the times you have set aside to work your business, and then work with total focus during those times. Set aside time to be with your family, and be fully present to them during those blocks of time. Allow your family to be part of your enterprise – together you will enjoy the journey!

How to Live in the Now

- When you are with someone, be fully focused on them.
- Concentrate on the conversation you are having; block out other thoughts.
- Schedule time for what's really important.
- Don't seek success at the expense of your family.
- Balance your future goals within the context of your whole life.
- Enjoy the journey.

13

Just Do It – A Call to Action

The world has the habit of making room for the man
whose actions show that he knows where he is going.
NAPOLEON HILL

Has there ever been a more successful advertising tagline than Nike's "Just Do It"? Twenty years ago, the newly created tagline received a lukewarm reception from Nike executives, who were on the losing side of a shoe war with Reebok. Today, the eight-letter phrase is among the two or three slogans rated most memorable in advertising history, and Nike has become the world's largest sporting goods company. Those three simple words, written by Portland advertising whiz Dan Wieden in 1988, symbolize clarity and practicality. The simple, powerful slogan moved beyond the world of physical fitness to become synonymous with forward movement – not just for athletes, but for anyone with a vision. People wrote to Nike saying that "Just Do It" had inspired them to leave abusive husbands and achieve heroic personal feats.

I'm definitely a "Just Do It" kind of guy. I'm the type of person who, when I get a thought in my head, I just do it. Anything that I've ever wanted to make happen, I just decided to make happen. This is both a good quality and a bad quality. It's good because there are so many people out there that never take action. They have great ideas;

they have a huge whys and desires, but they never translate these into action. The downside for me is that, for the longest time, every time a new idea would come along, I'd take action on it, which ended up being a real detriment.

You can read a million books on personal development. You can read every single book there is to read on *how* to do it and *why* to do it and *when* to do it, but the bottom line is that it comes down to you just taking one step forward; it's all about *you* taking *action*.

I can't tell you the amount of times I've heard people say that they can't do something. The word "can't" drives me absolutely insane. When somebody says, "I can't," what they're really saying is, "I'm afraid" or "I'm scared." They really mean, "I don't like the feeling that I get when I try something I don't know how to do"; "I'm afraid that it will give me pain"; "I don't know what will happen if I can't succeed."

People are afraid of pain. I always use the analogy of somebody burning their hand. If you burn your hand once, you're going to be very careful not to do it again. If you fail once, or some endeavor doesn't bring you the success you expected, you're naturally going to be gun-shy about ever attempting something like that again. If you burn your hand, you have every right not to want to burn your hand again. But you do not have the right to say "I can't" about something you've never attempted before. How do you know you can't until you've actually attempted it? It just doesn't make sense.

Network marketing is not that complicated; it's a simple business. It's not easy; it takes a lot of work. I've been through some of the worst pain in the world. I've made more mistakes than anybody else; I've lost all my friends in the process. But I realized in the darkest hours of my journey that there were people out there that have been through a lot worse. Look at the seven inspirational leaders and what they've been through. We all bleed the same way. We all breathe the same way. We all eat the same way. We're all human beings. We all have the same mind. And we all have the same potential to be successful. I look at Warren Buffett, Steve Jobs, and Bill Gates, and I think, "If they can have success, why can't I?"

Studying the seven leaders and identifying the characteristics that made them successful enabled me to realize my core task and keep focused on it. One step forward, day after day, and then I went to work on the other nine traits. You, too, instinctively know that if we all breathe, eat, and bleed basically the same way, then we must all have that same inherent ability to be successful.

Complacency Will Kill You

Earlier I talked about reading Joel Osteen's book, *Becoming a Better You*. Joel spent a lot of time talking about the hereditary link to one's current state of reality. His thoughts fit here with complacency also. If you are stuck in a rut right now, in may be a lineage problem, an environmental problem, or even a situational problem. The bottom line is this: You CAN change it.

Revisit the leadership continuum that we learned about in Chapter Three.

AUTHORITARIAN   COMPLACENT   INSPIRATIONAL

Dictator Ego-Driven Demanding   Procrastinator Indecisive Excuses   Caring Connector Heartfelt Inspirational

If you are in a complacent place right now, that truly is the worst place. You have to take action. But be careful, if you are stuck at complacency right now, it can be dangerous. If you decide to take action, according to the continuum, the first thing you have to do is make a decision. You can take a left turn and head in the direction where I found myself five years ago, an authoritarian ruling through fear, aggression, and belittling – or you can turn right and start on your own journey to inspirational leadership.

Now that you have read this book, you have no excuses. Decide to take action. Focus on the ten characteristics of inspirational leadership, and get ready for a life of prosperity and abundance.

Roadmap to Success

Start by identifying your core task, which in network marketing is prospecting. Focus on it, and then work on the other nine techniques. This will be your roadmap to success. But in the end, nothing matters if you don't take action. If you're not trying, you're dying. The success you're looking for is not a magic door; it's not Pandora's box waiting for you to open it. It's about taking one step forward. It's about trying different strategies and techniques. It's about practicing what you're doing, not worrying about the outcome, not worrying about the income, but just running as fast you can, always moving in the direction you want to go.

I hope that you decide to take action, to *Just Do It.* Remember what Gandhi said. That one simple phrase became the catalyst for me: "You must be the change you wish to see in the world."

I attended a training in Baton Rouge, Louisiana recently. One of the leaders I was working with said in front of a group, "The most important thing is the outcome." A thought jumped into my mind as he said that. **Our business is not about the *in come*; it's about the *outcome*.** The outcome is what you are really after. If your why is big enough, it will give you the motivation to take action. It's not about the income; it's about the outcome. This is a powerful statement.

Your ability to take action is tied to the reason you're doing this business. If your reason is big enough, you'll do it. It's like the story I mentioned earlier in the book about the woman who realizes her son is trapped under a car and just lifts that car up to free him.

A fourteen-year-old boy in Florida was despondent about not being big enough or strong enough to make the football team. Leaving practice early one day, he was walking home when he saw a car hit a pole and careen into a retention pond. The car began to sink, with an elderly driver trapped inside. Along with two other men, the young boy dove into the pond and swam some fifty feet to the sinking vehicle. Together they pulled the man from the car and swam back to the bank with him.

The boy later said that as he was watching the car sink, his instincts and what he called "a higher power" took over and "I just jumped in." He concluded that God wanted him to walk home that day rather than call his mom for a ride. The paramedics described the rescue as amazing, because the water was very cold, full of snakes and alligators. This is just one of many examples of people coming to the aid of a stranger, with no thought for their own safety. In the moment, they had a big enough reason to risk life and limb, and they just did it.

Everybody has the ability to take action. Every single one of us has the ability to go to work and to make things happen for ourselves. Those that aren't making things happen just haven't identified a reason big enough yet to move them to take action. Successful people in network marketing are those who have discovered a big enough reason, and they've allowed that reason to propel them into action. It's that simple.

If you want to be successful, you have to get your mind off of the money. That's tough when so many of us are struggling with debt and financial pressure. This makes it even more important to have a strong why – a very clearly defined outcome. All of us have areas that require improvement. Hopefully, you haven't been abandoned by all of your friends the way that I was, but that caused me to examine who I was. Next came a series of events in my life that caused me to study these incredible leaders, and from that I saw the characteristics I wanted to develop. I decided to just focus on those characteristics and let the results just happen. And they did! There's no reason why you who are reading this book right now can't take the same advice. You don't have to recreate the wheel. You can just follow what worked for me.

Once you get that core task perfected, focus on the other nine points. Become a better person; work on your own gravitational pull. Realize that life is about serving other people. Pay more attention to details, build confidence, and improve your communication. All of these things work together. And, of course, find a great mentor. Find somebody who has the success you want; find somebody that has the same type of personality that you aspire to have, and be willing to trust that person enough to take their advice. You'll become the inspirational leader that you w : to be. But nothing will happen if you don't take action.

I didn't write this book in order to become an author and make a million dollars and go on a speaking tour. I wrote this book for a couple of very simple reasons – as a public statement of accountability and to help find a cure for the disease that killed my dad. I am committed to continuing on the road to success myself. I've read many books over the years that have assisted me to develop this mindset. If you want to achieve the ultimate success you're looking for, then you must do what other leaders are doing. True leaders are always students; they're always reading, and they're always developing. At the back of this book, I've included a list of the books that have assisted me to make the profound personality changes I desired. Now that you have finished my book, recommend it to someone else and pick your next read from the list I've provided at the back.

Wake Up!

A friend of mine, Paul Rogers, is definitely one of the most charismatic people I have ever met. His passion for people and his ability to understand and care for others has impacted my life. He shared with me a poem that I'd like to end this chapter with. It was written in the 1800s by John Adams, and it talks about what can happen when you decide to "just do it."

> *One man alone can awaken another*
> *And the second can awaken his next-door brother*
> *And the third awake can awaken the town*
> *By turning the whole place upside down.*
> *And the many awake can cause such a fuss*
> *That they finally awaken the rest of us.*
> *One man with dawn in his eyes*
> *Multiplies.*

I know that you, just like me, have the ability inherently in you to be great. We are all born with the same unlimited potential. The difference between me and many other individuals is that I took action. I guarantee you that whatever challenges you are facing today, whatever roadblocks or hurdles, it can't be as bad as what I have been through in the past six years. Please don't be just another person that reads a book, puts it back on the shelf, and dreams about a better life.

We're All in This Together

One person with passion can move mountains. The passion that you're developing by listening, learning, and growing will be the key to your success in this business. Tell yourself today that you're going to take action, and that you're not going to stop until your goals are accomplished. You and the thousands of people that are joining your opportunity are not wrong. Together, a team will be built, an empire will be created around you – thousands of people that are using the products and the services of your company – and with that you'll get everything you want out of your business. You *can* make a difference. If you've never done this before, don't worry. Neither have I. We're all in this together.

I hope that my story has given you the courage and confidence to become an inspirational leader in your own world. If *I* was able to overcome the challenges I've shared with you in these pages, then nothing can stop *you* from overcoming whatever has been holding you back. I wish you much success and joy on your journey!

Recommended Reading

The Richest Man Who Ever Lived, Steven K. Scott

Becoming a Better You, Joel Osteen

How to Make People Like You in 90 Seconds or Less, Nicholas Boothman

Why Good Things Happen to Good People, Stephen Post, Jill Neimark, and Otis Moss Jr.

The New Professionals: The Rise of Network Marketing, James W. Robinson and Charles W. King

Your First Year in Network Marketing, Mark Yarnell

Good to Great, Jim Collins

How to Win Friends and Influence People, Dale Carnegie

Notes

Notes

Notes